Contemporary Lace for You

Jacqueline Callaghan
Membrane Rock, *2008*

Contemporary Lace for You

Jane Atkinson

Location photography by David Bird

Webfoot Books

Acknowledgements

This book is dedicated to Joy Cradock, the best of all aunts

Grateful thanks go to those who read my text and gave me their advice – these include my husband Terry, daughter Charlie, and friends Sarah Weaver, Denise Watts and Margaret Tappenden.

The professional team who worked on this book each contributed very special talents: Janet McCallum helped me work out what I wanted to achieve, and then worked far beyond the call of duty to put that into practice; David Bird turned photography into an adventure; Katherine James gave me the benefit of her eye for detail; and Geoff Barlow managed the production at home and abroad.

Thanks also to those who loaned their work for this project; to those who provided extra photography: Jacqueline Callaghan (frontispiece and Fig 2.26), Mark Dimmock (Fig 8.32), Peter Smith (Fig 4.1), Amanda Stevenson (Fig 1.1) and Michael Wicks (Figs 2.7, 8.20, 8.21 and 8.26); to Sue Porter at Slimbridge Wetland Centre for the teal footprint; to Ian McKeever and Sue Michie for allowing me to show images of their work; to Roger Vaughan for the loan of a camera lucida; to Peter and Jaquie Teal for their technical advice; and to Mary Hewson and Vivien Prideaux for help with dyeing. Thanks also to Gail Baxter and Ruth Doepfner-Wettstein for making up polar pieces.

The Lace Guild and the former Southern Arts supported my research and development with generous bursaries, including the appointment of Ann Richards as my Mentor in the case of Southern Arts; her advice was invaluable. I am also grateful to William Hall and Texere for support with yarns for research and teaching.

Thanks are due, too, to all the students who booked on courses and ran with my suggestions. I believe teaching has extended the scope of my researches far more than if I had worked alone, and has encouraged me to dig deeper into subjects that offered inspiration for lace design.

Introduction

Only very basic Torchon lacemaking skills are needed for most of the work suggested in this book. Indeed, a non-lacemaker recently attended one of my design workshops and learnt to make the lace she designed afterwards!

All that is needed is the ability to make a few pieces of Torchon, and enough practice to feel comfortable and familiar with the process so that you can visualise how you might translate a new pattern into a piece of lace. Have the courage to make mistakes, and learn to start and finish on your own by consulting books, if you do not have a teacher.

On-going studies at the Mayo Clinic indicate that mentally stimulating activities such as knitting (and therefore lace), carried out in middle age, bring a 40% reduction in risk of memory loss in later life. In addition, repetitive activities such as these elicit the 'relaxation response' which alleviates stress and allows the brain to set aside intruding thoughts, the Harvard Medical School Institute for Mind Body Medicine has found. So if you don't yet make lace, start now!

This book aims to turn a craft with a past into one with a future. Lacemakers know that they feel beneficial effects as they work at their pillows – I felt I 'saw stars' the first time I picked up bobbins, and I know that the day's stresses fall away when I draw my work towards me in the evening. Teaching at Central Saint Martins has shown me that bobbin lace is on the cusp of a revival, with many young people keen to learn how to get to grips with the technique.

Those currently working on the many other aspects that Contemporary Lace can take – Torchon being only one type – will be at the root of this resurgence. I would like to salute their work, and encourage you to seek it out on the websites recommended at the back of this book.

Contents

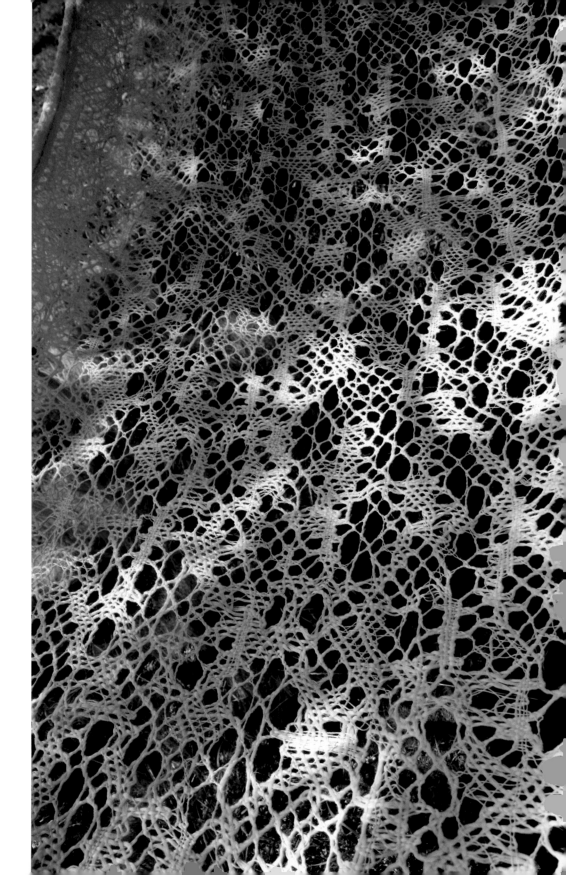

1

Contemporary Lace and You

New impetus for an old lace

Traditional bobbin lace uses fine threads and much repetitive labour to produce fabric of great intricacy. Contemporary lace gives new life to this venerable old craft, combining lace skills with new ideas and materials to create fabrics that reflect the tastes and values of modern life.

This new lace presents a fascinating opportunity to mix colour, light and filament to form intriguing and beautiful works of art such as sculpture, wall-hangings, textile jewellery, home furnishings and clothing, and release the spark of creativity present in us all.

Fibres from other textiles and filaments from industry may be used if the structure is adapted to suit them, and virtually any fibre may be wound onto bobbins, while cords, cables and wire may be coiled.

Work may fill an architectural space or adorn the body as a delicate piece of jewellery. New technology takes lace beyond textile when electroluminescent wire structures react to human presence, or fibre optics build delicate patterns in space.

However, yarns from weaving, knitting and embroidery can be used to create lace at a scale accessible to all, lace that may also be made at far greater speed than traditional forms. This book outlines how to realise this using Torchon, one of the simplest styles.

Torchon is a widely made lace, usually white and designed on a square grid, popularly used for household trimmings. Yet its uncomplicated and flexible construction makes it eminently suitable for development in the most dynamic of ways.

The Torchon grid may be stretched, expanded, distorted, warped and curved, yet still remain simple enough for work in a variety of scales. The wider the grid is spread, the faster and more rewarding work can be. It also allows the incorporation of coloured and textured yarns that conventional scale often denies.

The effects may be vibrant and exotic or direct the focus towards textural properties in a subtle way. Contemporary creations can be attractive, desirable, commercial and personal, an exciting and enjoyable form of self-expression capable of much improvisation, enabling us to conceive and make pieces that suit our individuality.

The broad set of interrelated skills contained in this book may be used for designing new work as well as for the more personal interpretation of existing patterns. However, unusual effects are often easier to achieve if we design especially for them than if we try to adapt a traditional pattern.

Fig 1.1 *Far left: Betty MacDonald Torchon jacket, 2008 Wool and mixed fibres*

Fig 1.2 *Above: Betty's design planning*

Fig 1.3 *Below left: Jane Atkinson Samples for the braid made by the author to complete the jacket, 2008*

Betty MacDonald, a talented artist, printmaker and needlepoint tapestry designer, was already designing exciting and individual work. A course in contemporary Torchon, held at her home in Philadelphia, inspired her with the possibilities in large-scale and textural work. Enlarging logarithmic patterns found in *Pattern Design for Torchon Lace*[1], she used a Chanel jacket paper pattern as the basis for a lace jacket made from knitting and tapestry yarns (Fig 1.2).

Her beautiful and adventurous project (Fig 1.1) was not without its challenges: 'I started at the top of each piece and ended at the bottom edge with lots of threads to tie off,' explains Betty. She is now making another jacket 'the other way up' and tying off the threads as she moves upwards.

'I wanted to use lots of colours and textures in logarithmic patterns,' says Betty. 'A jacket was something I would really end up using. I've had a great time with it. I'm thinking I'd now like to do a silk blouse, but I haven't yet figured out how to make it lacy without being see-through'.

Lace for your lifestyle

Inspiration and design often work hand in hand. One of the most attractive aspects of designing for ourselves is the way it allows us to find creative inspiration from our own environment. In order to show how we can build on previous experiences to generate new ideas, we will start by looking at the development of a series of experimental pieces.

This new style of Torchon lacemaking is hugely versatile. Grids themselves can help to generate new ideas; once we have examined the potential in the best of existing grids, we can move on to the development of expressive new ones. These can be fitted to modern threads for the creation of distinctive and dynamic pieces of lace.

Learning how to design with and for the wide variety of yarns currently available enables the lacemaker to plan and make innovative and exciting pieces of lace. If we know how to test and evaluate the best of these yarns, and perhaps change them to better suit our purposes by dyeing them, we can attain real control of the process.

Adding colour to the old geometric laces was always complicated, but colour can become much simpler to control once one understands how threads work through patterns. With a little planning, threads may quite easily be organised to deliver beautiful and intriguing results.

If we add some knowledge of colour perception as applied to textiles, and learn how to use the laws governing pattern and symmetry to our own advantage, we can then turn our ideas into reality with the design of original patterns.

We can generate new designs in several ways. Unique motifs for geometric Torchon may be generated by using simple toys which quickly allow our creative ideas to flow, such as pattern stamps. The wonderful patterns waiting to inspire us in nature may be translated to suit modern tastes for abstract design, while more representational work can be created with the stylisation of flowers and foliage.

Each new lace design project brings its own challenges but there are always practical solutions for solving problems. We must choose the right equipment and decide how to match our individual skills to the task. For example, it is perfectly possible to design without having drawing skills and there are many advantages to using the computer to create our own source material. We can even create lace without a pattern. This book also addresses the practicalities of starting and ending work, and finishing pieces professionally.

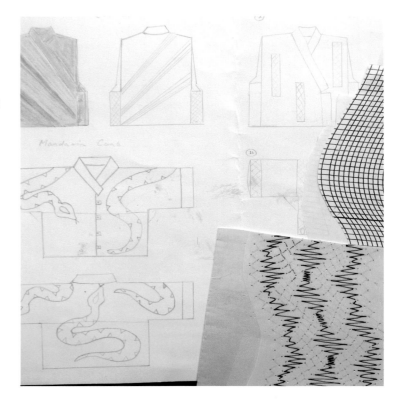

Fig 1.4 *Top right: Jacket designs*

Fig 1.6 *Right: Lace experiments*

Fig 1.5 *Below: Snakeskin inspiration*

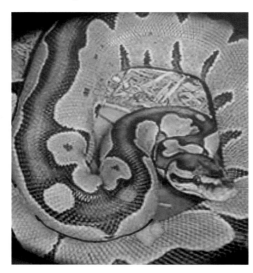

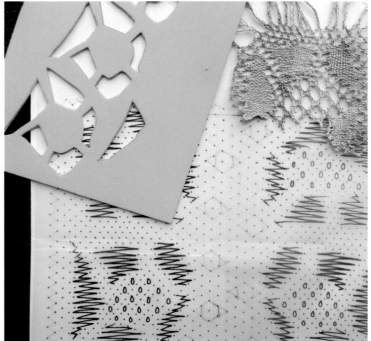

Pauline Denmark, a former Lace Guild chairman, found that contemporary lace gave her a whole new direction after traditional work became too trying for her eyesight.

'The only limitation is one's imagination,' says Pauline, whose 'light-bulb moment' came during our discussions about creating a 'body of work'. The design process is an important part of the time taken to bring a project to fruition, and Pauline realised that if she could do a variety of designs on a theme (Fig 1.4) she could select fragments to make into a succession of items.

The jacket pictured here (Fig 1.7) is one of a series embellished with lace warped and patterned with ideas taken from snakeskin (Fig 1.5). Since then, Pauline has designed a range of accessories, including spectacular hats and fascinators incorporating contemporary bobbin lace.

'For years, I had wanted to make "commercial" lace which might be desired by any woman,' she explains. 'Until that discussion, I had not thought about using the design process to make more than one item. That was the route to being commercial. This realisation gave me a huge sense of freedom.'

Fig 1.7 Right:
Pauline Denmark
Black and gold silk
jacket, 2006
Trimmed with lace in
linen 16/2
Author's collection

2 The Creative Process

Building on experience

Being creative is a journey, but we can never tell where we'll end up.

In order to demonstrate the way that projects evolve if we let our creativity motor, this chapter describes how an idea developed, over several years, into a series of lace pieces, changing form as each phase revealed new possibilities.

The creative process involves:

- Observation
- Preparation
- Incubation
- Inspiration
- Realisation and
- Verification.

Craft work is a learning spiral, where we often revisit aspects of our project a number of times but on each occasion with greater depth as experience accumulates. In a 'body of work' (related pieces on one subject) this experience works to our advantage, spinning off into a variety of solutions. It is important to accept that this should not be rushed; lace is a time-consuming business but we may need to take as long to create the design as to make the product.

Let us look at what each stage involves.

Observation: the more deeply we involve ourselves in design, the more receptive we become to the stimuli that lie all around us. Collecting anything likely to be useful in the future and responding to the Zeitgeist become second nature.

Preparation: once focused on a subject, this involves researching in books, on the internet, drawing, gathering photos and cuttings, experimenting and thinking.

Incubation: making the right connections between what we want to achieve and our present level of experience may mean leaving new information to mature while the subconscious mind resolves the problem.

Inspiration: this involves the energising moments when those connections click and a way forward becomes clear. Inspiration may come while doing something totally different – taking a walk or relaxing in the bath; this is, after all, where Archimedes got his *Eureka!* moment.

Realisation: this is the practical effort to prove that the idea can actually be made – working with the chosen tools and materials, solving problems and learning lessons. It involves rendering the form so as to bring out a particular conception or meaning and making up or interpreting a pattern in one's own personal style.

Verification: here we ask ourselves whether the product works to our satisfaction and, most importantly for an artwork, whether it communicates its meaning to others, and is valued by them.

We can use the creative process to our advantage by keeping several projects going simultaneously at different stages, preparing one while thinking about another and making something else. Being creative is about finding novel solutions to new challenges.

If an impasse occurs, prop the work up and leave it for another day; simply viewing it with an open mind later on may be enough to trigger a fresh insight. We all have an inbuilt ability to recognise patterns and to group configurations into 'organised wholes' – psychologists call this Gestalt. It enables us to see the whole picture, taking in continuity, symmetry, similarity, proximity and closure (where we complete a figure even if it has a gap in it).

Gestalt theorists call the shapes that stand out in the foreground 'the figure', and the context that gives the figure its meaning 'the ground'. It is interesting that these words connect so well with lace.

Fig 2.1 Left:
Bone Lace II; Swept
Away, *2007*
Texere rug warp and
Czech linen
183 x 91 cm

Bone Lace

So let us look at the process in action. In this case study we will follow how a chance *observation* triggered a personal response that led to the creation of a series of pieces I called *Bone Lace*. If we can use our own experiences of life and the insights these have given us, we can create work with greater impact.

One of the hazards of ageing, often ignored by younger women, is the onset of 'brittle bones' from the condition known as osteoporosis. The condition had wrecked the lives of several close relatives (including the aunt for whom I had been caring) and made me acutely conscious of how fragile and vulnerable our bodies are.

Some years before this project started, I had picked up a leaflet from the National Osteoporosis Society (NOS) which showed photographs of the condition (Figs 2.2 and 2.3). For a contemporary lacemaker, the striking thing about the illustration of thinned bone is its similar appearance to lace. When some friends and I decided to hold an exhibition on the theme of 'Rhythms and Cycles', I decided to explore this relationship in more depth.

In addition, I hoped I could use large-scale contemporary lace to highlight the importance to women of taking active steps to ensure bone health throughout their lives.

After trying to make lace that looked like the structure of bone, several life-sized works emerged, which became metaphors for the difficulties which the condition brings as items of relaxation and comfort become symbols of discomfort and pain.

In the process, I moved from a free lace interpretation to completely new ways of improvising with Torchon.

Casting the net

Since it is good to cast a wide net around a problem, part of my *preparation* involved a response to a photograph of strong bone in the NOS leaflet (Fig 2.2). This reminded me of knitting, but experiments with linen and needles proved how much easier it was to improvise with bobbin lace. Knitting random holes involves a two-row process which needs detailed knowledge of the subject, whereas bobbin experiments can be made over the top of a graphic; an expert knitter also remarked how stable my bobbin experiments were, in contrast to the way knitting would roll.

Abandoning that idea, my attention focused back onto the thinned, osteoporotic bone structure (Fig 2.3). A tiny image from the leaflet (the most graphic demonstration of the destruction wrought by osteoporosis that I could find) was enlarged on the photocopier many times so that I could study it, eventually ending up 40 cm / 16 in. wide. The image showed a complicated 3D filigree which I decided to convey with two interacting layers of lace. For the first layer, I highlighted and traced the front of the bone slice (Figs 2.4 and 2.5), and for the second I explored the partly

obscured underlying structure, imagining how it would have joined together (Fig 2.6). Since Torchon would have been too regular for this, I decided to make the layers in free lace.

To capture the stiffness of bone, the yarn also had to be strong and stable. The stiffest yarn available at that time was Texere rug warp, available in three sizes (see yarn charts pages 134–37 for all yarns mentioned). Following a Czech method detailed in Jana Novak's *Moravia* books, pairs were hung into a plait along the top. The threads were worked in interconnecting sections of half-stitch around the edge, splitting up with plaits and twists around the holes in the design. Threads were hung out from a plait at the end, and cut short after being oversewn with one strand of the yarn, to give a neat appearance despite the thickness of the yarn.

Making lace around large holes needed considerable ingenuity, which prompted thought on the condition itself. Patients with the condition are given bone-building drugs, but rebuilding must be hard to achieve from a depleted structure.

Bone Lace I, Vertebra (Fig 2.7) was the first piece for the 'Rhythms and Cycles' exhibition.

Fig 2.2 *Below left: Healthy vertebra*

Fig 2.3 *Below right: Osteoporotic vertebra*

Fig 2.4 *Right: Exploring the photo*

Fig 2.5 *Centre right: Layer one*

Fig 2.6 *Bottom right: Layer two*

Fig 2.7 *Far right: Bone Lace I, Vertebra, 2006 Texere rug warp 39 x 43 cm*

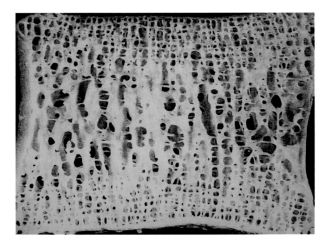

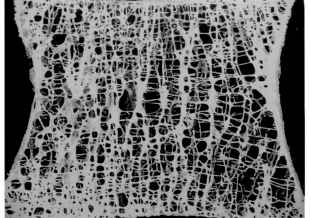

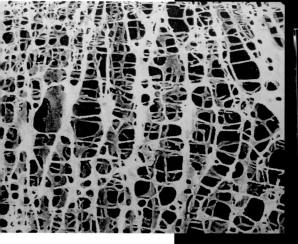

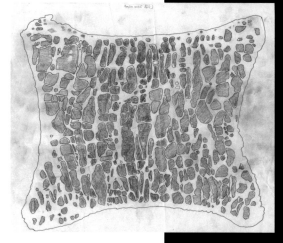

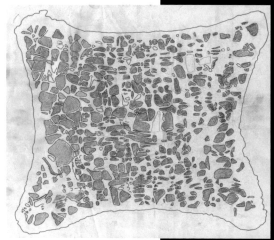

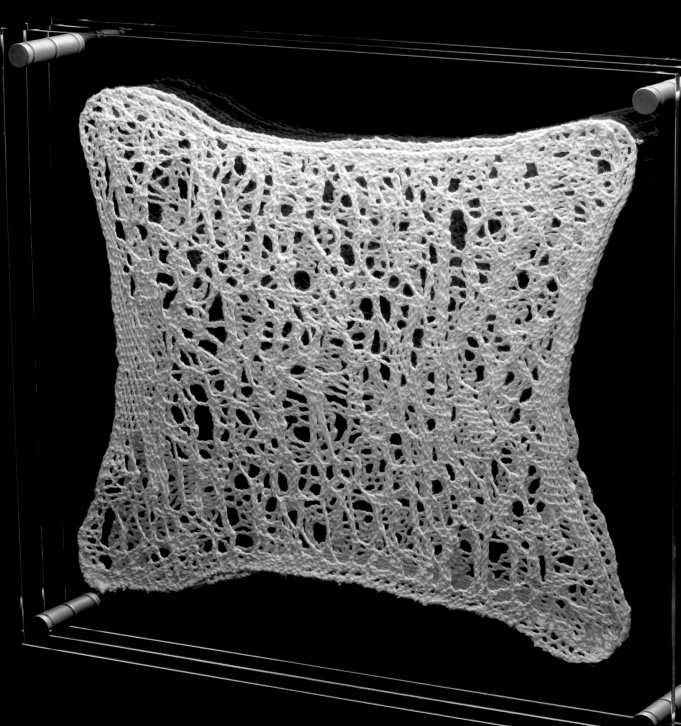

Awaiting developments

So far, I had drawn an analogy between lace and thinned bone, but the purpose of the project was to highlight the effect the condition can have on the rest of life. Healing slows down with age – a young person's broken leg will heal in a few months, but for an elderly person this can take far longer; in the case of my aunt (after two falls), a whole year. Tough lifestyle decisions may arise, including facing up to the fact that independent life may need to be replaced by constant care.

I let my bone lace take a back seat for a while, leaving things to *incubate* whilst tracking the progress of my aunt's recovery in a sketchbook diary. I came back to it from time to time, wondering where I could take it next.

The tragedy of osteoporosis is that the bone structures on which we have always relied fail to support our body, so that we have to rely on other support 'structures', medical and personal. My aunt now seemed to be stranded – the analogy of a hammock came to mind, strung beyond reach of solid ground. Could I make one using the bone construction I had explored?

The free lace method would be difficult to pursue with this sort of challenge, involving lace up to 91 cm / 3 ft wide; Torchon would be easier, if one could find a way of replicating the informal pattern of the bone structure.

Sketchbooks are part of the artistic process and I wanted mine to be full of background information for the exhibition. In order to make it attractive, I decided to stencil its blank pages, so photocopied the first piece of lace and enlarged it as the template (Fig 2.8), then cut it from card (Fig 2.9). When explored using Brusho inks, the stencil became sodden, printing itself, some of which was too intriguing to cover up with anything else (Fig 2.10). The template was used as the cover and the stencil itself became the starting point for an abstracted Torchon pattern (Fig 2.11). By tessellating a portion of the pattern (see page 98), it would be possible to spread the design to the required width (the working surface of the largest available pillow) and to any length.

Rather than compromising this big piece of lace with loops and attachments, I decided to add a straight edge, the pattern being in kit form with the edge added as required (Fig 2.12).

However, even abstract Torchon is a regular process, so the technique needed to be flexible to reflect the irregularity of the bone.

Whereas the first free lace experiment had been risky but fun, involving thinking on one's feet, samples of the new pattern were boring, both to make and to look at; this was something I just had to overcome. Could some lateral thinking help me? Conventional lace restricts work to one thread at a time; perhaps I could use a variety? Other threads could include different thicknesses of rug warp as well as doubled 16/2 weaving linen and a Czech linen with quite different properties, smooth and tightly twisted as against the loose and fibrous rug warp.

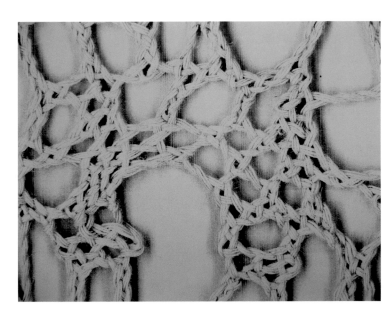

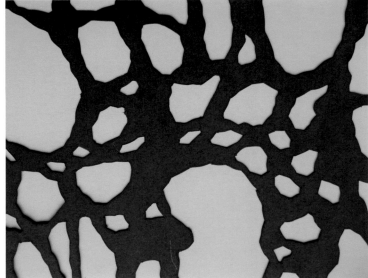

Fig 2.8 Far left: *Enlarged lace photocopy*

Fig 2.9 Left: *Cut stencil*

Fig 2.10 Right: *Sketchbook page*

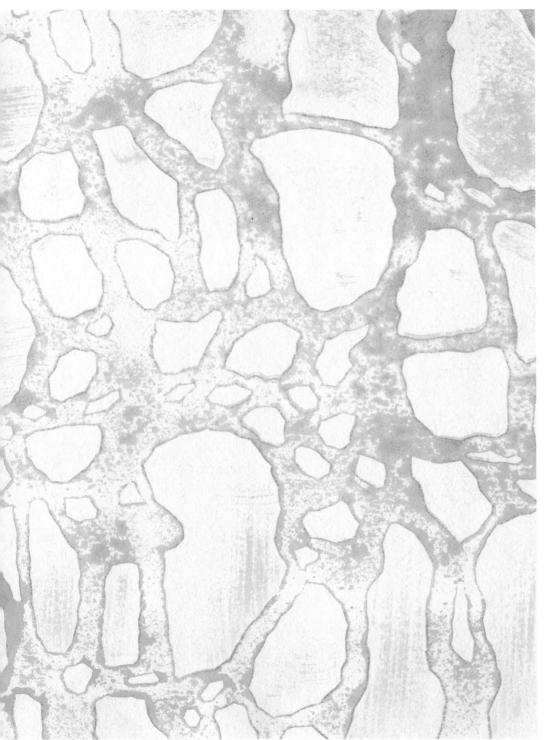

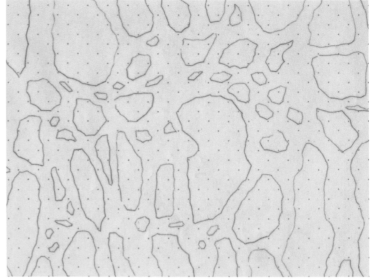

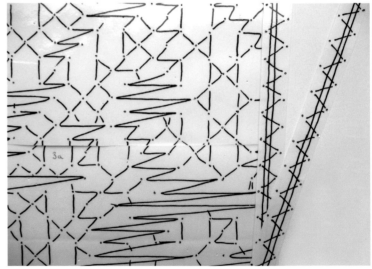

Fig 2.11 Top:
Stencil shapes with
grid: the pattern was
drawn between the
holes

Fig 2.12 Above:
Pattern kit

11

Thinking through change

Changing our thinking patterns can help us to negotiate mental blocks. De Bono suggests that instead of thinking 'vertically', we need to try 'lateral' thinking.

What is the difference?

The **vertical** thinker:

■ checks new ideas against objective criteria
■ moves only if there is a direction in which to move
■ is sequential
■ has to be correct at every step
■ uses negatives to block off certain pathways
■ excludes what is irrelevant
■ fixes categories, classifications and labels
■ follows the most likely paths
■ settles for the first solution
■ considers that rightness matters most
■ selects pathways by excluding others
■ selects the most promising approach.

The **lateral** thinker:

■ discovers new directions of thinking in the quest for new ideas
■ moves in order to generate new directions
■ can make jumps
■ does not have to be correct
■ does not use negatives

■ welcomes chance instructions
■ does not set categories and labels

■ explores the least likely paths
■ is probabilistic
■ considers that richness matters most
■ seeks to open up new paths
■ generates many alternatives

Moments of *inspiration*

Even in a greater variety of threads, the first gridded lace sample did not convey the strongly horizontal/vertical structure of the bone. Another sample was made with half-stitch and whole-stitch blocks but looked too heavy (Fig 2.13). Lighter threads were added and the whole-stitch abandoned, but it became too light and featureless (Fig 2.14). My planning was evidently not working, being too prescriptive to allow the frequent shifts and changes in texture necessary to give the lace the appearance of the real bone. Perhaps it might be possible to allow the threads themselves to dictate the stitch textures?

Where thick threads emerged together from the half-stitch mix, they could be allowed straight runs down the pattern in whole-stitch (Fig 2.15), this process also giving opportunities for horizontal emphasis where suitable. This would keep me constantly on the alert, looking ahead and gauging possibilities, but within known parameters. It would be an intriguing game to play, using a few

Fig 2.13 Below left: Sample 2, whole-stitch and half-stitch

Fig 2.14 Below: Sample 3, half-stitch in lighter threads

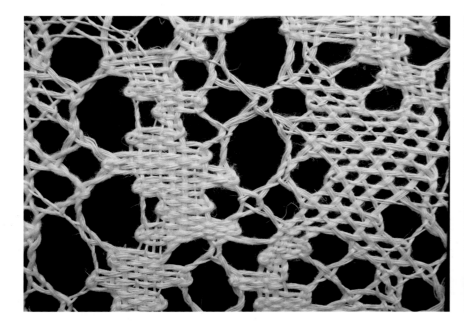

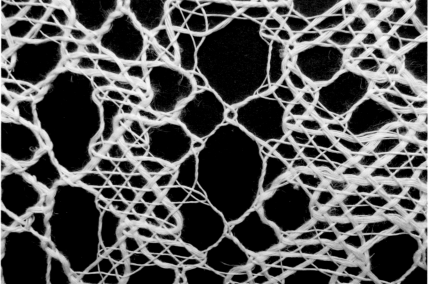

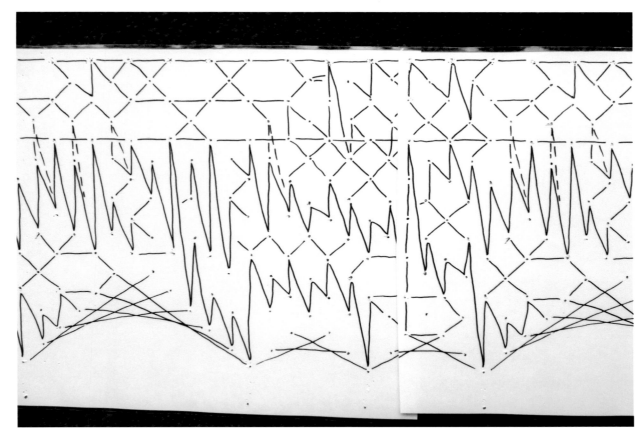

simple rules to keep life interesting and challenging, but simple enough to sustain for the 2 m / 6 ft length.

Part of the pattern was adapted for hanging side-pieces, again in kit form to allow a pattern with fairly random interpretation and points for tassels to be added at irregular intervals (Fig 2.16).

At this point, with the basis of a design clearly established, it was important to think seriously about construction and display. The piece would be hung in a huge room where display might be difficult, so a stand would be useful. Hammock-ends were also likely to be tricky, and this was researched.

The department store John Lewis provided the answer, offering a hammock with stand precisely the same size as the one about to be constructed. Its canvas was attached by loops of tape to stretchers strung on sturdy rope, which then hooked into the stand; the solution for this project was to create a webbing harness to carry new ropes and attach to the stretchers, into which the lace could be sewn (Fig 2.17).

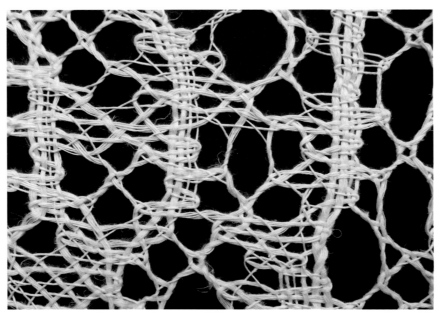

Fig 2.15 Left: Sample 4, with vertical features

Fig 2.16 Above: Side-piece

Osteoporosis is not just a question of broken limbs; the impact of walking may be enough to cause the bones in the spine to collapse. This leaves the sufferer in constant pain, even when sitting still.

How could I show the pain of sitting? What simple seat could be made from lace?

The visit to the department store offered the solution. I was able to buy a deckchair with a removable canvas that could be replaced with a lace one.

The objective was to highlight the discomfort being felt when sitting by transposing it onto the new deckchair 'canvas', effectively plotting a chart of my aunt's pain.

This 'pain chart' was sketched onto a scaled diagram of the seat and then enlarged 500% as the canvas pattern

(Fig 2.18). The task then was to create an openwork fabric strong enough to take the weight of a real body, for this was going into an exhibition where a visitor might possibly decide to try it out; both hammock and chair had to be able to function as real furniture.

The fabric should have a regular rather than a crafted appearance, and the design was constructed in tapes to replicate commercial canvas stripes but on a regular, gridded format to allow interlinking where red stripes might spread through the work to represent the pain (Figs 2.19 and 2.20).

The way forward was now clear to *realise* both projects, as a three-part series on the subject: vertebra, hammock and deckchair.

I still felt there was extra potential in the hammock design and an international lace festival at Vamberk, Czech Republic, presented the opportunity for further exploitation.

Narrow strip-scarves had recently come into fashion, and these were an ideal subject, being small and swift to make and hence economic to sell.

The basic hammock pattern could

Fig 2.17 Below left: *Hammock construction detail*

Fig 2.18 Below: *Pain diagram drawn by the patient, Joy Cradock*

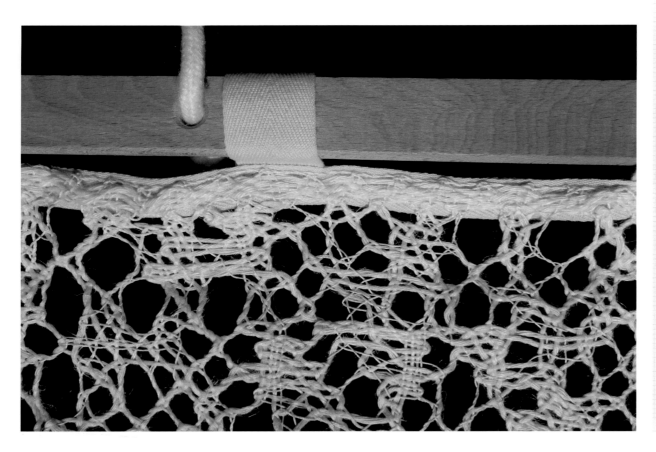

easily be sliced into strips and worked in a scale suitable for 16/2 linen (Fig 2.22).

Several colourways were explored, including one in the various shades of natural linen that are produced by the different countries still processing it – Ireland, Poland, Sweden, Finland, Germany and the Czech Republic. According to climate and process, these vary from creamy beige to almost grey.

Working the different threads together gave an ideal test-bed, the Polish thread proving far stronger and stiffer than its gauge led me to imagine (Fig 2.21). This opened up the opportunity for the pattern to be pushed beyond the dot-pitch normally suitable for thread of this size, spreading this delicate pattern wider and allowing a larger scarf to be made more affordably.

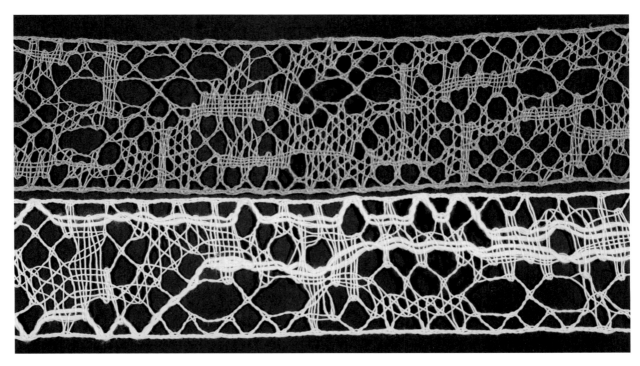

Figs 2.19 and 2.20 Below: Deckchair samples

Fig 2.21 Above: Polish linen used in scarves

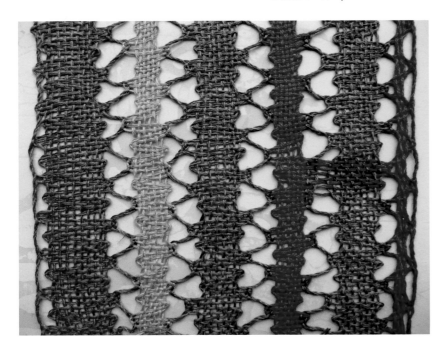

Greater exposure

Among other textured threads found at Vamberk was a rough, tough thread with a pronounced sinuous nature. Thought to be hemp, it made an excellent though subtle contrast with the smooth Polish linen. Once back home, a wider scarf was quickly constructed in time for the main exhibition. It was largely based around these two threads, with the Polish thread providing the basic structure, and a few others added to give different textures (Fig 2.23).

As all the pieces were now ready for the exhibition, the focus turned towards publicity material. It became apparent that whilst those visiting would hopefully get the message, after the show was over another medium would be required to give wider visibility. If a work of art cannot be seen, it cannot convey its meaning to an audience. As the pieces would not be on permanent display, I turned to photography. Through photographs, the work could live on – on the web and in books or magazines – giving a greater exposure of the message.

With this objective, the photographs had to be more than just publicity material; they had to have an impact all of their own. The photographs themselves had to be works of art.

Professional photographer David Bird was keen to add his own creativity to the process and, after taking the lace pieces 'on location', he produced a highly expressive set of images.

The point of the project, enhanced by the photography, had been to connect with younger women visiting the exhibition. The hammock at first shocked a middle-aged osteoporosis sufferer, and then motivated her to continue with bone-strengthening exercises: 'If I don't feel like going to the gym, I remember the hammock.'

The piece became part of another photographer's creative vision when, a year later, Jacqueline Callaghan was looking for pattern-making and lace that related to the body. Faced with lace that 'encompassed both notions with a depth and conceptuality I had not envisaged finding', she responded by including it in her series *Horror Vacui* (Fig 2.26).

This project has explored the way we can take an idea, turn it into lace and push further to give our craftwork the exposure it deserves. It has shown that we need to be flexible and patient while the creative process takes its course, to adapt to changing circumstances and take inspiration as it surfaces, wherever that might be.

The lace techniques used in the *Bone Lace* project were very basic. I had not worked free lace before in the manner used for the vertebra, but experience in Czech-oriented tape lace (where one often responds spontaneously to a very sketchy pattern) had been particularly appropriate.

The process proved that Torchon's grid system is highly versatile as a way of spreading surface pattern, and if we move beyond existing technical confines then we can incorporate far more light, shade, texture and informality than when sticking to the rules. Equally important is a greater knowledge of fibres and yarns in order to use them to their best advantage, both in traditional white and in colour.

These skills, an understanding of grids, familiarity with fibres, confidence with colour and relaxation with rules, are all easy to acquire. They will give your lace a greater impact as an artistic medium; they will speed up your lacemaking and give you the incentive to move forward.

Fig 2.22 Left:
Strip scarf collection, 2007–08
Linen from various countries
Approx. 152 x 10 cm

Fig 2.23 Right:
Bone Lace scarf, 2007
Polish linen and Czech hemp, with others
150 x 21 cm

Creativity in Action – Going with the flow

David Bird had already had experience of capturing his wife Rebecca Newnham's mosaic sculptures in the landscape, and never seemed to go anywhere without observing and assessing locations for possible future use. He suggested photographing my deckchair on the beach at Milford on Sea with the Needles, a string of chalk stacks on the end of the Isle of Wight, in the background. Half an hour squirming around on the beach to find the right angle at which wind, waves and location would give the piece his best shot ended in disappointment (Fig 2.25) but it led to something much more meaningful.

Eventually David shifted his sights away from the Needles and just had the chair forlornly in the shallows, as if abandoned (Fig 2.24). This brought the comment from my deeply interested aunt whose pain was being charted: 'All washed up, just like me.'

Fig 2.24 Left:
Bone Lace III, Are You Sitting Comfortably?
2007
Linen tow 4 and linen 16/2
111 x 43 cm

Fig 2.25 Below:
On the beach.
The Needles are the rock formations on the horizon

Fig 2.26 Right:
Jacqueline Callaghan Precipice, 2008

Creativity in Action – In the blink of an eye

Jacqueline Callaghan was nearing the end of an MA in Fashion Photography at the London College of Fashion. Looking at how clothes relate to the body and at man's relationship with the natural world, she was considering 'how insights might be drawn from assessing body adornment practices common to all cultures. The human process of pattern making soon revealed prominent parallels.'

Working on the subject of *Horror Vacui*, she was looking for lace design that addressed serious issues, and was intrigued to find that in my *Bone Lace* project I was working on a life-and-death subject with strong links to her own.

For her, making the final piece was not a process like lace which could take weeks to implement, but one realised in a few milliseconds as her shutter snapped. To choreograph the image she sought – in a wild environment, against the vagaries of the late autumn weather, with a nude model and assistants positioning lace over a rocky chasm – she spent days working everything out beforehand.

'As a photographer I am concerned with constructing a surface pattern with three-dimensional objects. I cannot escape – and do not wish to – from the very literal definition of photography as "drawing with light".

'When I am observing or creating an image the first thing that I am struck by is the arrangement and tonality of the elements as a whole; this is the key: to feel the rhythms of an image which can lead to subconscious insights.'

3

Grids by Art and Artifice

Fig 3.1 Left:
Grids off the peg –
decorative wrapping
papers

Fig 3.2 Below:
Ian McKeever
Assumptio, 1997–98
Oil and acrylic on
cotton duck
245 x 330 cm
Private collection,
Russia

From here to infinity

Torchon lace is based on a square grid, usually deploying geometric pattern designed over graph paper. More sophisticated patterns, such as those in Point lace, are drafted on a hexagonal grid which is better suited to flowing design.

In both of these cases, the underlying grid is 'passive', serving only as the platform on which design takes place. By designing our own grids, we can add an extra layer of creativity: an 'active', expressive new structure with which to add impact to our lace.

Grids can take many forms – once conscious of them, we can find them everywhere. They regulate the layout of the page you are reading, the stacking of the box in which your book was delivered, the design of the building that stored it and the supply of the electricity that powered the printing press. Grids, whether flat, 3D or metaphorical, bring order to our lives.

Many modern artists have used dynamic grids as the heartbeat of their work. For Ian McKeever (see Fig 3.2), fragile and nebulous gridded ribbons of white paint are part of a visual language which offers 'structures which mediate between what I might be and the wider world beyond … neither vertical nor horizontal but floating' [2].

Drawing up individual grids allows us to 'warp' the basic structure to make our lace more dynamic. We can start by using the grids we find as we go about our daily lives, for example those printed on wrapping papers (Fig 3.1). Using these new grids will bring liveliness to our lace without making it any more complicated to produce.

Contemporary lace exists in a borderland between craft and art. Experimentation with its underlying platform can give lace dramatic visual impact for both utilitarian and artistic purposes.

The grid in modern art

The expressive use of grids appeared early in the 20th century, but became especially popular in the latter half. The energetic black-and-white Op Art patterns of Bridget Riley became a hallmark of the sixties, but she has continued to use contrary patterns of visual motion throughout her career to create mesmerising, vibrating sensation.

Minimalism added 3D structures, modular and geometric grids, drawings and paintings to this vocabulary – even a famous pile of bricks.

Critics such as Rosalind Krauss suggested that the grid – which can draw attention to its centre or impel the viewer to the edge, suggesting progression to infinity – had become a purpose in itself.[3] Lucy Lippard detected that the repetitive work involved in much female needlework, but particularly in the wrapped and gridded processes used by Eva Hesse, showed 'ritual as antidote to isolation and despair'.[4]

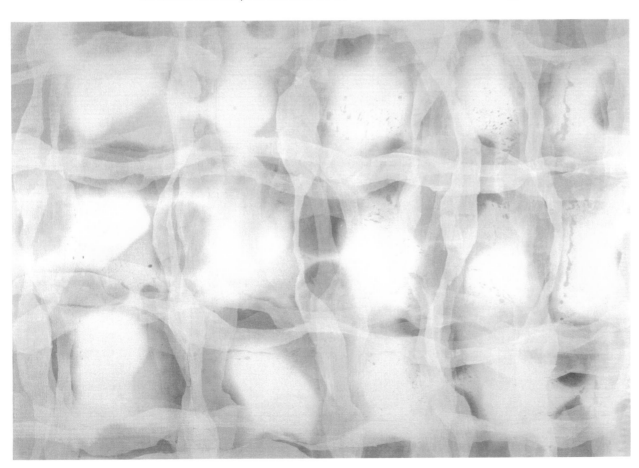

Hand, eye and heart

Drawing our own grids will take us into new territory and can be an absorbing and fulfilling process in its own right.

We can set ourselves the task of delivering perfect, machine-like uniformity or we can work to let in chance and hazard, delving into the unknown for beauties yet to be revealed.

For the lacemaker, generating a new grid will be the groundwork for the creation of a textile design, but there are some artists, such as Susan Michie, for whom it can be the goal itself.

Susan sometimes uses a grid for her dot, line and dash drawings, which prompted fellow artist Simon Lewty to observe: '… the grid in its masculine aspect appears as a figure for imposing order and uniformity upon the world', but 'it has a feminine side too, as an image of relatedness without hierarchy and of integration within the world'.[5]

Susan's tiny repetitive marks slowly build up on the paper as she works: 'For me the act of repeating a movement, a line, a simple mark, contains a memory of thousands of years of women's work. It is the mistakes that make my images, something a machine or computer is programmed not to do. It's the tension between trying to control the marks and allowing them to go their own way that makes the surface an organic one.

'In a case such as *The Protecting Veil*, I start with a straight line and try to repeat it down the page but being human, of course, it's impossible. The wiggles and waves begin to occur and that creates the image.'

Although Susan's images are hand-generated, some could be taken for natural patterns from rock, wood or water.

Starting with the mark she has chosen for the work, she allows its symmetry to be 'broken' by events: her breathing, the movement of the muscles in her arm, the repetitive process. This can accumulate into glorious patterns at its resolution,

in the same way that the malleable substance of nature breaks down as forces act upon it.

The process may also be beneficial to the artist: 'I may be angry about something in the morning, but as the day goes on, the laborious activity allows my mind to wander and to think the problem through from different points of view,' Susan admits.

Ernst Gombrich suggested that 'the art of drawing … is rooted in the soil of natural organic movement. If every draftsman did not have his own personal rhythm, his own handwriting, the connoisseur's effort of attributing drawings to masters would be hopeless.'[6]

Working with pencil in hand is a physical process where the sweep of the arm is our compass of reference and 'the mark always carries an autograph'.[2] The feedback of hand and eye offers total flexibility; often a machine will only allow actions someone else has already pre-planned.

*Fig 3.3 Below:
Susan Michie
The Protecting Veil,
2003
The title pays homage
to a piece of music by
the modern classical
composer John Tavener
Ink on Saunders
Waterford paper
300g/m
51 x 165 cm*

*Fig 3.4 Right:
Detail of The
Protecting Veil*

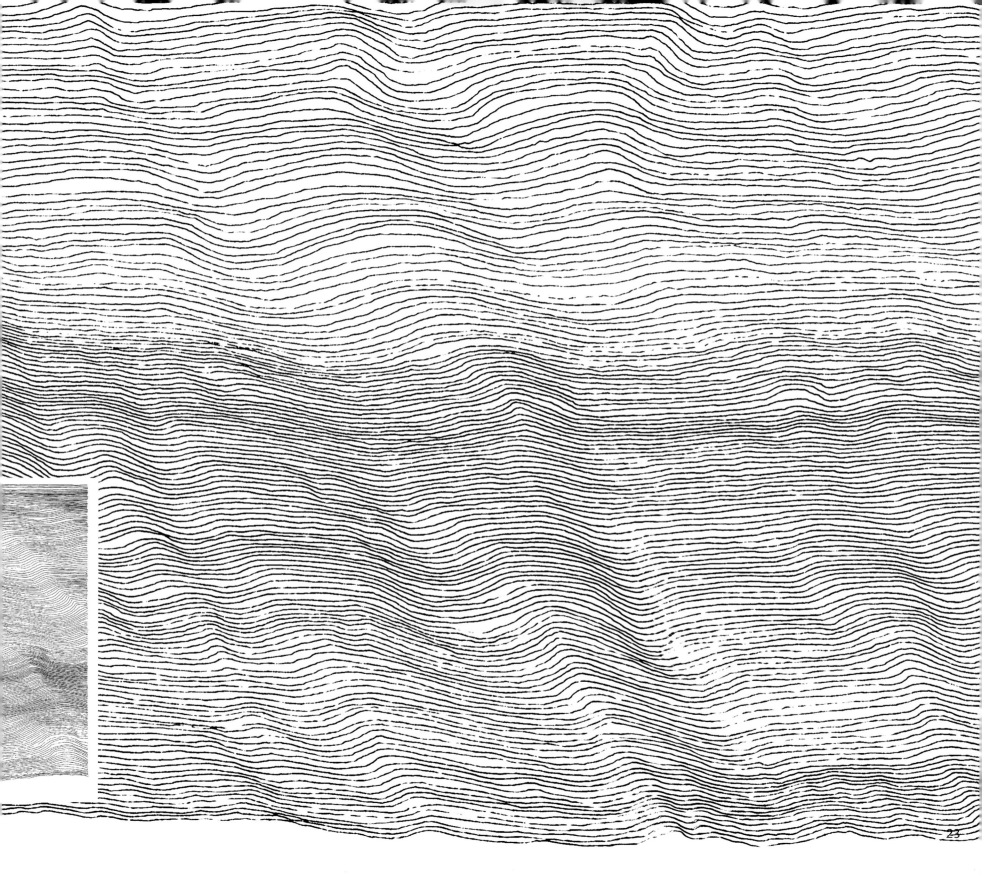

23

Commercial grids

Before exploring personal grids, we need to be comfortable with the design process on squared paper.

Professionals in the commercial world still start drawing by hand, even if the result is then transferred onto a computer. Car designers, for example, may start with a hand drawing, then produce a clay sculpture before the computer takes over; architects will sketch before computer modelling.

Grids can be downloaded from the internet, but I prefer a pad of lightly printed graph paper so that I can draw my design clearly over it.

Graph paper scales (metric or imperial) and paper sizes differ from one country to another and it would be sensible to use whatever is easiest to find, adapting the lace design process to it. Special grids dotted for lace, such as Plotadot (see page 139), now with a wide range of options, make it easier to choose whatever best suits our pattern or choice of thread (Fig 3.5).

Selecting the most suitable graph paper involves consideration of the size of the pattern and the thread to be used; for a traditional-scale geometric pattern that might be made up in 40/2 linen, 1/10th, ½, 1 in. may be a good choice, but for general-purpose design doodling perhaps using the cheapest may be more appropriate (2, 10, 20 mm may often be bought from surplus stock stores).

In larger scale (for scarves and hangings), it is sensible to work on a 1 cm grid and then enlarge on a photocopier to the size required to suit the chosen thread (see pages 134–37). This helps you avoid pitfalls such as too much or too little detail, or creating a design that is incompatible with the tools and equipment to hand.

When designing patterns abstracted from nature, either lay a transparent grid over the source design, or lay a traced design over a paper grid. Transparent grids may be created by photocopying grids onto tracing paper or dotting them by hand. They may also be bought on tracing paper (for maths, knitting or embroidery), acetate (OHP) and plastic (as knit leader sheets).

Large dotted grids for heavier pieces may be created by tracing off sheets of dots from large sheets of printed graph paper – one good tracing will last for years and may be photocopied *ad infinitum*. The photocopier does add a slight distortion, but its benefits usually outweigh the disadvantages.

Designing by methodically joining up dots or drawing corner to corner over a grid can be a quiet pleasure. Pattern motifs may be drawn up as solid blocks, and the dots traced off straight from the grid (Fig 3.6); or we may transfer one repeat to the computer and work on it there.

To complete a pattern, many different edges and foot-sides may be culled from old designs, or you can make up your own. *Pattern Design for Torchon Lace* gives more detailed suggestions for geometric pattern drafting.

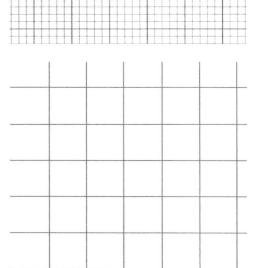

Fig 3.5 *Right:*
Commercial grids available in various countries
Top row, across both pages:
Sizes: 2, 10, 20 mm;
1, 5, 10 mm;
5 mm;
4 mm, European.
Middle row:
1 cm;
¹/₁₀, ½, 1 in.;
⅕ in. US;
¼ in. US.
Bottom row:
Knitting grid;
Martina Wolter-Kampmann diamond 5.5 mm;
dressmakers' ¼ in. grid;
Plotadot grid

Fig 3.6 *Below:*
Tracing a pattern motif

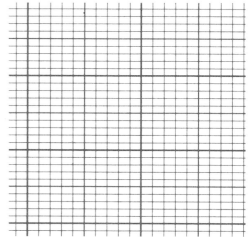

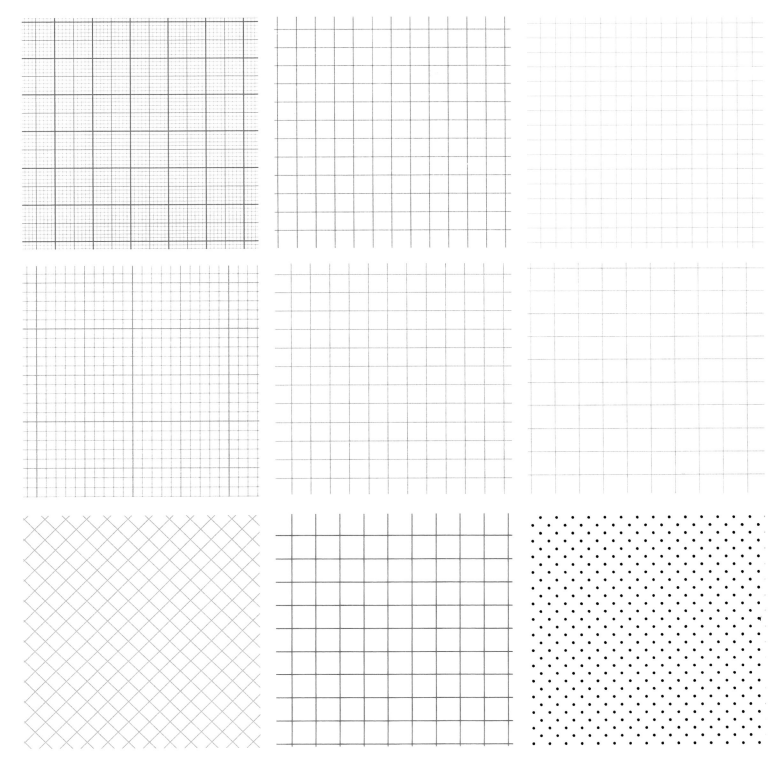

Logarithmic (log) grids

Logarithmic grids are used to simplify complex mathematical calculations; parts of these offer non-linear instead of regular spacing, which can put flowing movement into lace patterns.

Although not so often needed nowadays, there were many kinds of printed log grids produced for science and engineering before computers became ubiquitous, and these may still exist if you ask around. For lacemakers, special log grids are available which have design aids built-in.[7]

To start designing with a log sheet, hold it horizontally at eye level and squint along the dots to examine the curves they produce; drawing along them will show ways of making patterns that use the bend and flow of the grid to best advantage. Exploring the basic symmetrical skeleton of the grid by drawing in the dividing lines between repeats and dividing them diagonally to find the centres, as has been done with the new Plotadot versions, will give extra

understanding of where to plot pattern elements to best advantage.

One grid may offer different options on how to make a design work; in the two by two-way symmetrical pattern illustrated (Fig 3.7) it might seem natural to work from top to bottom (a), but working around four quadrants would use half as many bobbins (b).

To find out what the lace would look like before you make it, interesting colourways and plans may first be traced in fibre pen; time spent exploring options will save thread and lacemaking effort. In the examples shown here, half-stitch ground would facilitate the quadrant version (b) and whole-stitch ground is the key to the vertical one (a), although the threads still work the pattern motifs in the same colours.

A chance gift of some large log grid sheets provided me with the basis for a large-scale project where long and attractive runs of gradual increments allowed wide areas to be created in honeycomb or virgin ground.

These grids, when layered in *Under*

the Red Bough, 'interfere' and shimmer as moiré patterns when the viewer walks past. Pieces that interact with the viewer in this way are known as *kinetic*. Kinetic art is a whole movement on its own, where movement is inserted by artist or audience for different effects.

Log grids give a new twist to simple shapes, whether the desire is for them to be bright and vibrant or in subtle pastels. The work of the Hungarian-born, French-based artist Victor Vasarely (1906–97) can inspire both design and colour usage, which may be used to accentuate the illusions created by the fluctuating grid (Fig 3.10).

Grid size may need to be adjusted to the chosen thread. The variations in dot-pitch require the selection of thread that is soft enough to be compacted in dense areas yet sufficiently strong to support open areas. Most suitable is pearl cotton, which comes in extensive colour ranges and several counts, coloured linen, and lightly twisted filament silk (which may be plied on the bobbin although it could need protecting under glass).

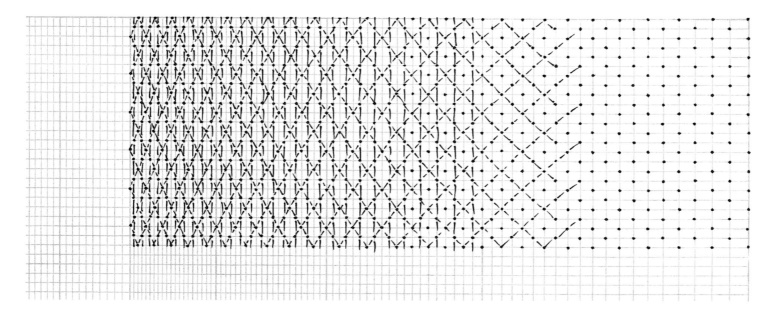

Fig 3.8 Left: Creating a honeycomb lace grid from a large log sheet

Fig 3.7 a, b Right:
*Options for
interpreting one
pattern*

Fig 3.9 Far right:
Under the Red Bough
I & II, *2004*
Bockens 16/2 linen
146 x 62 cm

a

b

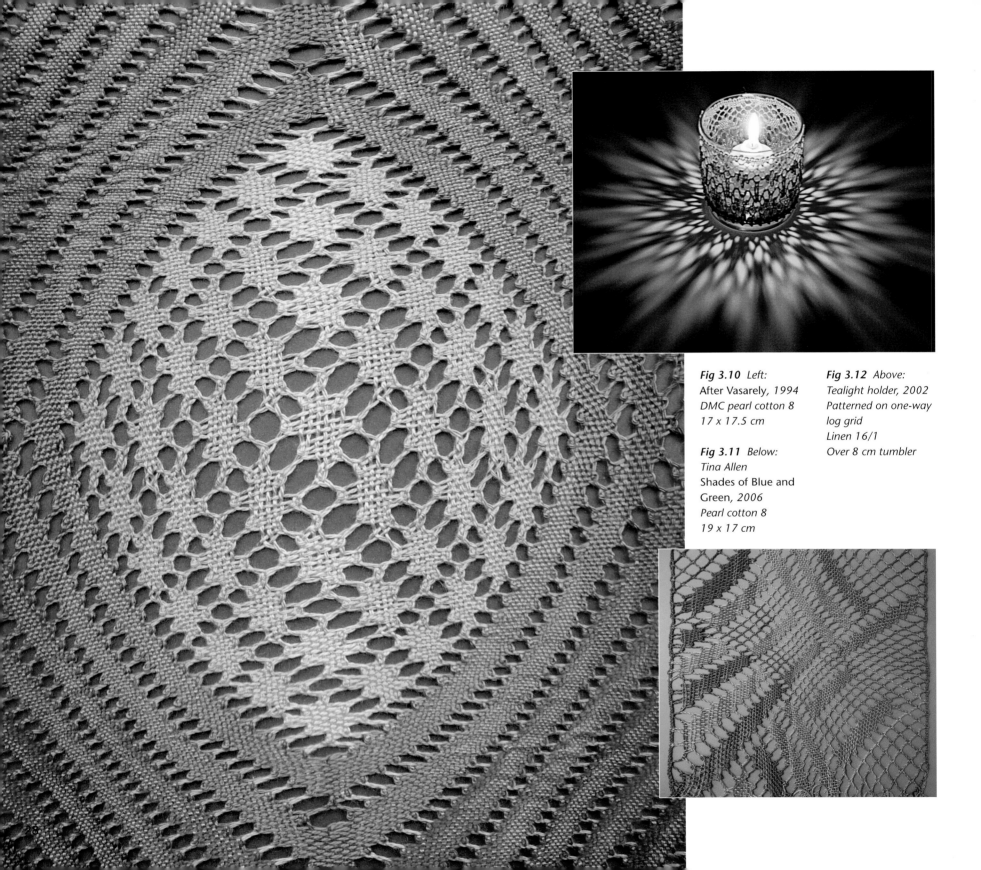

Fig 3.10 Left:
After Vasarely, 1994
DMC pearl cotton 8
17 x 17.5 cm

Fig 3.11 Below:
Tina Allen
Shades of Blue and
Green, 2006
Pearl cotton 8
19 x 17 cm

Fig 3.12 Above:
Tealight holder, 2002
Patterned on one-way
log grid
Linen 16/1
Over 8 cm tumbler

Polar log grids

Polar log grids spread intriguing dot-pitch variations around a circle with sometimes complex results. Those published as A4[8] can benefit with enlargement to A3 or similar, and then need exploring to find their parameters. Patterns will have slower or faster rises according to dot-pitch and grid flexibility.

Joining up a diagonal line of dots will give an idea of the possibilities on offer; these can be very attractive and quite extreme. The number of dots around the circumference may split usefully into four quadrants.

Some of these grids include sections where the dots are very close together. Avoid putting too much detail in these areas or pins will be too close for comfort. It may be preferable to design over these areas to get around the constrictions.

Talented designers have made the most of polar log grids in some sophisticated work. Designs over dense grid may require considerable perseverance to work, and such effort is well rewarded.

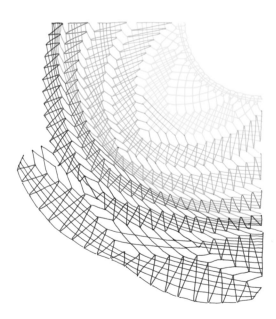

Fig 3.15 Left: Joan Wakem Amaryllis, 2005 Cotton Finca 16 27 cm diameter

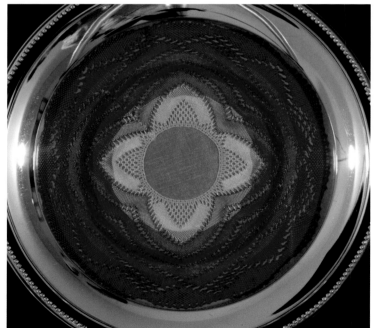

Fig 3.13 Far left: Thread chart

Fig 3.14 Left: Polar log c. 2001 Pipers 3fold 90 silk floss 15 cm diameter First pub: Lace Express

Fig 3.16 Below: Amaryllis flower

Polar grids

Polar design (now possible on Plotadot grid) can be really satisfying because it allows us to create pattern that draws the eye around a circle to give dynamic movement. A yard-lace design translated into a circle may be completed swiftly in a limited number of repeats.

Polar work can be an excellent place to develop and evaluate design skills, allowing strategies to be explored for extrapolation elsewhere. The basic grid has 90 dots around the edge, which may be divided up into two, three, five, six, nine and ten repeats, but there are now other variations, as well as quadrants or quarter-circles which may be joined for large circles or fans.

The choice of number of repeats depends on the motif and the effect required; the more repeats, the busier the pattern. If we transfer a polar design to the computer, we need to remember that it must remain a workable project and a satisfying design. For instance, the computer might allow us to modify a pattern from six repeats to seven, but that could give extra work and upset the balance of a symmetrical design.

The dot-pitch of a polar grid varies between the inner and outer edges, which will demand careful thread selection, but there are a number of solutions. If the design is suitable, different threads can be used in different parts of the pattern – finer threads towards the centre, thicker ones in the outer area. This can allow a change of shade, or the use of different thicknesses of the same thread; fine ones, such as filament silk, may also be plied to suit.

Extra threads can be added to the edge, extra colours introduced to make motifs (just hang them out at the end of the motif), or bulkier stitches used (braided instead of Torchon grounds).

Polar designs can also be made in delicate threads if the finished piece can be mounted under glass. The yarn charts on pages 134–37 offer thread suggestions.

Design strategies such as paper-cuts, layering tissue or translucent paper, design toys (stamps, mosaics, Spirograph, Kaleidodraw, Playstano, kaleidoscopes, French curves etc.), floral shapes, antique designs, architectural ornament and the transfer of existing border patterns can all play their part here.

Once the number of repeats has been established, their boundaries should be marked on the grid to show exactly how much space each contains. It also helps to mark in the inner edges of the border fans to see the outer limits of the design.

Circular silver or steel trays are an excellent vehicle to display polar lace, especially if destined as a gift. In this case, mark the size of the tray aperture on the grid to indicate the limit of the pattern before you start to design.

Straight patterns gain new life as circles, and circular designs may also be modified into fans.

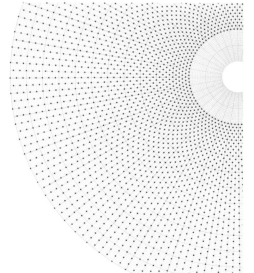

Fig 3.17 *Right:*
Polar patterns
Linen, cotton, silk,
1988–2008
Up to 27 cm diameter

Fig 3.18 *Left:*
Polar grid

Fig 3.19 *Top:*
Mini fan leaf designed
from polar pattern
Both linen 40/2
23 cm diameter
First pub: Lace Express

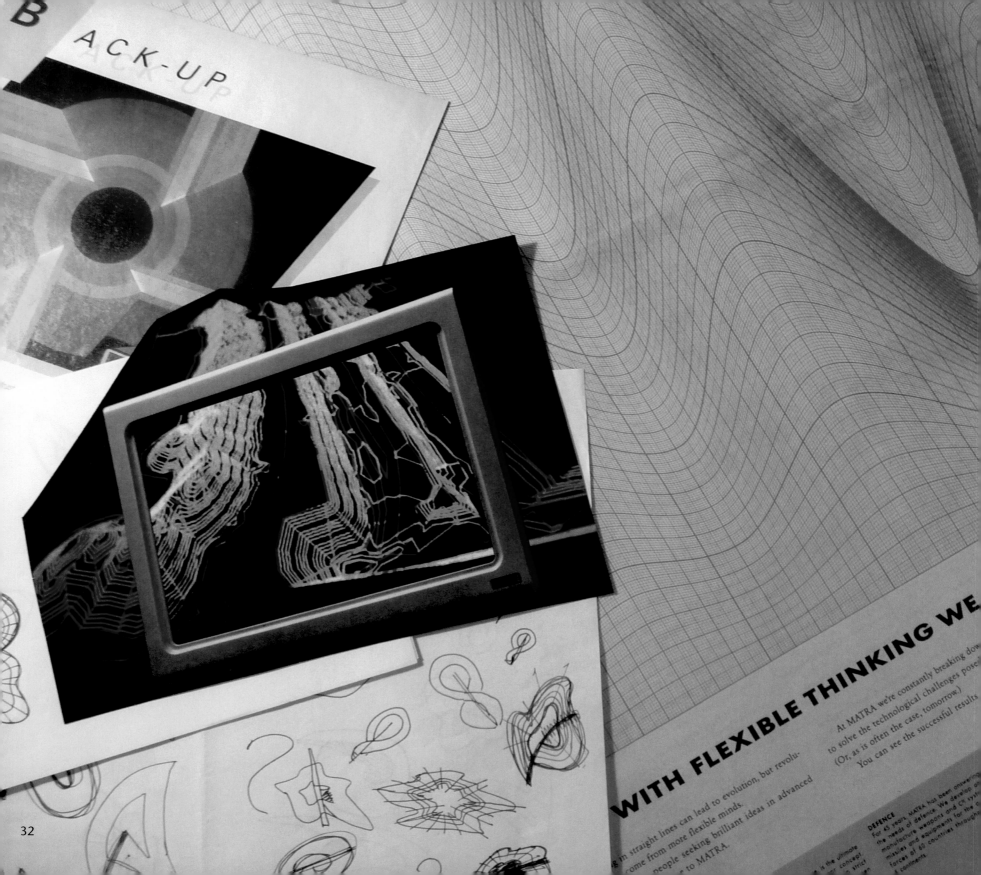

BACK-UP

WITH FLEXIBLE THINKING WE

At MATRA we're constantly breaking dow
to solve the technological challenges pose
(Or, as is often the case, tomorrow.)
You can see the successful results

g in straight lines can lead to evolution, but revolu.
come from more flexible minds.
people seeking brilliant ideas in advanced
to MATRA.

DEFENCE
For 45 years, MATRA has been answering
the needs of defence. We develop an
manufacture weapons and C3I syste
missiles and equipments for the a
forces of 60 countries throughou
4 continents.

32

Warped grids

Shaped or warped grids can turn simple lacemaking into something faster, more interesting and very useful. Instead of having to make yards of lace trimming, half a dozen repeats can make a necklace; three can make a shaped bookmark; one makes a Christmas bauble. Once created, a new grid can have endless uses.

It was my husband's electronics magazines that set me thinking: an advert for a floppy disc controller (Fig 3.20, pink disk top left) had concentric rings of colour – so could threads be sent round a piece of lace in that way?

Since threads travel diagonally in Torchon ground, circular motion seemed impossible, but parallel lines offered possibilities. Designs based on diagonal lines of coloured silk were explored in crayon and a pattern was drawn so that the drawings could be translated into lace (Fig 3.21).

Other electronics literature expanded the concepts; an advert for the French engineering company Matra contained a flexible grid of such a high quality that I could probably have used it for lace. However, another advert for a flexible printed circuit, the kind that is curled into electronic goods such as cameras, suggested a contoured grid.

I used this in my search for a shape that could be twisted so that the end would be in a different place from the beginning. This was to avoid the problems, for instance in polar grid, where threads have to be sewn into the starting point and colours must match. With the warped shape, colours could be schemed without fear of the consequences. At first, because we may only have a few colours, colour schemes may be limited, but as we collect more colours, more sophisticated choices become possible.

The instructions on the following pages show how easy it is to:

- create a useful shape and *mould* a grid inside it
- create a *flowing* grid and then find a use for it
- tailor an expressive grid to a fluid subject.

In a subsequent chapter we will look at the use of computers in finding designs for lace. It was, after all, computer-aided design (CAD) that first gave impetus to my own grid-drawing experiments. Experienced and properly equipped computer users may prefer to undertake many of these processes on their PC or Mac.

However, we will confine ourselves here to learning how to do it by hand; indeed, the attempted use of CAD may stifle our creativity. A contemporary lacemaker commented on viewing one of my pieces: 'I tried to do that on the computer but I couldn't manage it.'

Fig 3.20 Left: Inspiring grids from electronics adverts and the doodles inspired by them, which matured into the designs on the following pages

Fig 3.21 Right: Red/Green/Orange, 1984 Piper silk 300/4 floss 20 cm diameter

Fig 3.22 Far right: Initial thread design

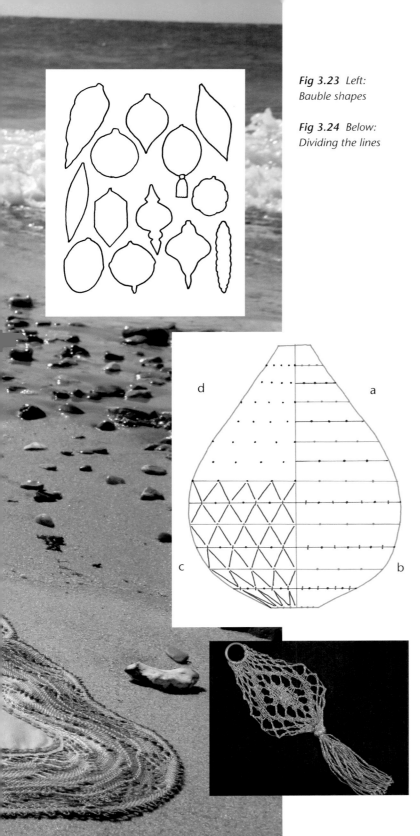

Fig 3.23 Left:
Bauble shapes

Fig 3.24 Below:
Dividing the lines

Moulding grids 1: to spaces

First we will look at filling a shape with a moulded grid. This works for large subjects as well as small ones. For more complex pieces, just divide the shape into simple portions and tackle each in turn.

These grids are easy to produce by hand and eye; they may need refining – join up the dots and re-align if the lines wobble – but this can be quickly achieved. Moulded grids may also be modified and extended.

To create a simple, symmetrical, Christmas bauble:

1 Fold thin scrap paper and cut bauble shapes to find one you like (Fig 3.23).
2 Draw around the edge of the shape, on plain or graph paper, and work on half to begin with.
3 Draw horizontal lines 5 mm / ¼ in. apart, or fold the shape in half several times to find them. With a pencil mark, divide each line in half, then half again (Fig 3.24a).
4 Divide alternate lines in half again with a slightly different mark (Fig 3.24b); the grid is created by joining these secondary marks with the ones in the line above (Fig 3.24c).

5 Trace off the grid and copy the second half by turning the tracing paper over. Refine the grid if necessary, and draw in a simple design.

Hung into a curtain ring and finished with a knot to make a tassel, these baubles take just a couple of hours to make. Adding 26 gauge wire on the edge (twisted on each side in opposite directions to keep it flat) will allow flimsy but flashy yarns such as Goldrush to be used to great effect.

Such shapes may be repeated end to end and made into a galloon for trimming clothing, blown up large for thick knitting/ weaving thread, or reduced down for a bookmark in fine silk, which may be further embellished with tiny tassels.

I used the same process to create the grid for some double-centred mats (Fig 3.27), inspired by the doodles shown on page 32. Using a grid spaced for 40/2 linen, each section was handled methodically in turn. As different motifs were explored with lace, and threads were shown to take distinctive paths, subtle effects were seen to be possible. The pattern was then reduced to allow the use of mother-of-pearl colours (pale blue, mauve, pink, peach, yellow) in finer cotton.

Fig 3.25 Below left:
Bauble

Fig 3.26 Right:
Galloons and bookmarks

Fig 3.27 Main photo:
Mats in a moulded grid, 1988
Linen 40/2 and 16/1, and DMC Fil à Dentelles
27 x 32 cm

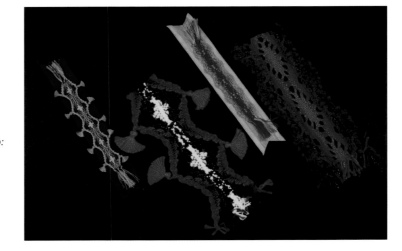

Moulding grids 2: necklaces

Wearable objects, such as necklaces and collars (Figs 3.30, 3.31), can also be based on a moulded grid. Once mastered, the method described here can be applied to simple and more exaggerated shapes and is viable for both smooth and acute curves (although the latter do require extra care).

The basic shape shown was created by drawing around a serving dish, with a pudding basin as a neck-hole (Fig 3.28). The shape was then modified to suit placement on the body.

However, cutting a necklace shape from a sheet of folded tissue paper to suit the neckline of a favourite dress, or just according to whim, are also good starting points. Practice will soon confirm where to add (with sticky tape and tissue) or subtract (drawing with a fibre pen, then cutting) to create a shape that works well.

Fold the result into sections and draft each section in turn. Only half the grid needs to be constructed and traced; it may then be photocopied from both sides of the tracing and the two orientations joined together. A good grid has endless uses, not least that it may be drafted with different dot densities for use with different threads and design effects. The right-hand side of the diagram (Fig 3.29) shows a wide grid, while the spaces between the dots on the left-hand side have just been divided one more time.

Exaggerated edges may be added as the design is drafted (see page 116), and the grid may stand as a skeleton for further exploration with distantly related shapes. New interpretation possibilities often suggest themselves as work progresses; the pattern you have added may send threads in a particular way around the piece, which then shows potential for more striking variations.

Back stitches in the centre of the pattern will allow the thread paths to unroll symmetrically to the finish, as in the large necklace (Fig 3.31). A dense grid in such a large project would have made the lace time-consuming to complete, but it became far more viable with a wider grid and thicker thread.

For fastenings, silver split-rings can be linked to construct a chain, and bolt rings, toggle clasps or hooks added according to taste.

Weight can be a problem with textile jewellery, because a light lace necklace will shift when worn. One solution is to add beads to the edge to weight it; these may be added afterwards but are ideally added in the making with sewings – threading them on at the start risks them not being on the right thread when needed. For a more dazzling effect, crystals, shell beads and semi-precious stones, as well as glass beads, may all be used to add weight.

Necklaces may also be made in metallic thread and fine wire, but weighting the front edge still remains important.

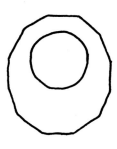

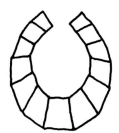

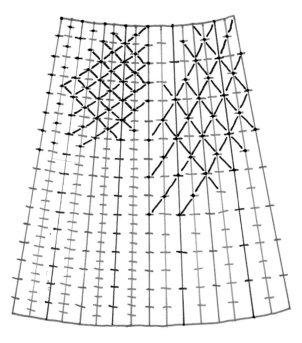

Fig 3.28 Far left: Basic shape for necklace collection, then modified for wear

Fig 3.29 Left: Different grid densities from same grid

Fig 3.30 Main photo: Necklaces, 1989–2008 Linen 40/2, cotton, metallic 31 x 25 cm

Fig 3.31 Inset: Large necklace, 2003 Linen 16/2 53 x 45 cm

Moulding grids 3: spirals and 3D

Other grids may be elaborated from nature. Even if the grid is curved, the basic process for fitting grids to shapes still applies, although the drawing and division of the intervening lines will be more testing. The project on this page was inspired by X-ray photographs but the shell section shown here is much easier to see (Fig 3.32).

The three *Nautilus* pieces illustrated were explored on different grids. The first, patterned with markings from the outside of a shell, was on a curved grid which developed intriguing properties by the time it reached the middle (Fig 3.33). At that point the threads were running at a very acute angle. This made the finished lace so unstable it could be expanded like a string bag.

The project was redesigned using a straight grid to make the lace more stable, but took much longer to make, the grid having unintentionally been drawn much more densely.

The third design spread the grid out wider, reducing the time needed from four working days to two and a half. Whereas the amoeba-shaped pieces on the previous page took ten days for the lace to be made and a further two to mount, the new pieces could be made much more economically and involved no mounting, only finishing.

The dot-pitch varied widely, but the problem was overcome by inserting extra twists in the ground or, in some places, by including thicker thread.

In pieces like these, which are complete entities that finish in a different place from the start, a mixture of colours may be used. Colours for the first *Nautilus* were chosen from the natural shades of the shell and for the other two were inspired by paintings. These designs could also be enlarged for thicker thread.

Three-dimensional shapes may also be gridded and shaped – for example, cone-shaped candle lampshades throw delightful shadows. The one shown here (Fig 3.37) was designed from a card shade given away in an interiors magazine. Finishing was completed over a padded roll, and happily the regularity of the pattern allowed most of the thread colours to match at the join.

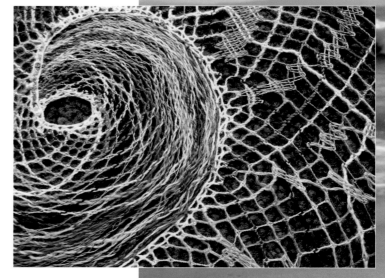

Fig 3.32 Left:
Nautilus shell section

Fig 3.33 Top:
Curved grid detail

Fig 3.34 Centre:
Expanding the curved grid

Fig 3.35 Right:
Nautilus pattern

Fig 3.36 Main photo:
Nautilus *mats, 1989*
Linen 40/2 and 16/2
27 x 38 cm

Fig 3.37 Far right:
Lampshade, 1989
Linen 40/2, Madeira
metallic 15
11 cm wide

Fig 3.38 Main photo: Saoirse *scarf, 1996 Plied DK cotton and Vuorelman 4 linen 122 x 26 cm*

Fig 3.39 Left: Marcel, *1994 Linen 16/2 with verticals in knitting and embroidery threads 183 x 28 cm*

Below, l to r:
Fig 3.40 Moving the template over the square, and drawing up the grid

Fig 3.41 Saoirse *pattern*

Fig 3.42 Starting point for Saoirse

Flowing grids 1: horizontal and vertical

Flowing grids developed from time spent drawing to music. Starting with the rise and fall of a repeated musical phrase, sound and sight gradually worked together.

If a flowing grid is drawn inside a small square or rectangular area with equal graduations along the sides, we can tessellate these (see page 98 and symmetry operations on pages 82–83) in various ways to extend the grid over wider areas. All that is needed is a piece of scrap card or a flexi-curve. Large grids can be drawn with a quilter's calibrated Flex-a-Shape design curve.

The following instructions are for a small example (Fig 3.40), but if you have a Flex-a-Shape, try it at a larger scale (I use 1 cm calibrations):

1 Cut a wavy line along a piece of thin card, and mark 0.5 cm / ¼ in. calibrations along the side. Any wavy line will do and you might get more selective as you see the possibilities develop.
2 Draw a square on some gridded paper and mark regular graduations along the sides. Make sure your piece of card is at least twice as long as the square.
3 Count the number of graduations on the square and mark at least that number in from the left-hand side on the card.
4 Lay the card so that one mark touches the first graduation, and the other end of the card touches the top mark on the other side. Draw the line.
5 Move the card on one space, and draw the second line at the next two marks below. Continue in this manner with successive lines.
6 Stop before the bottom if the line is likely to go over the edge and draw

the last one or two by eye, evenly within the space that is left so that they gradually flatten out towards the edge. Go back and do the same at the top if necessary.
7 Trace this series of lines and lay it at right-angles to the first series. Trace that, and you have a fluid grid.
8 Trace or photocopy more examples, and tessellate to contemplate.
9 To turn this into a Torchon grid, join the corners of each small section and dot off all the intersections, but keep the underlying grid in view for designing, to avoid getting lost (place a traced, dotted grid over the basic line grid for reference).

There may be many variations: squares may be drawn as parallelograms with wavy edges; the internal grid need not progress across but may stay in the same vertical orientation; two different sets of curves may cross, or one set may be straight lines; large squares may be cropped into rectangles.

Marcel (Fig 3.39) had one highly curved set of grid lines crossed with a gentle one, and the grid was developed as a honeycomb grid with threads chosen to enhance the effect. Stable threads like linen are preferable, but a scarf in softer threads can be blocked (see page 130) to regain its shape.

Saoirse (Fig 3.38) crossed one set of grid lines twice but was then cropped to isolate the most interesting areas (Figs 3.41, 3.42). One factor in the cropping was the available size of photocopier for enlargement. Working A4 and enlarging to A3 kept the process economical. The threads in the gridded sections were doubled cotton and linen, with the pattern lines in DK cotton. Shorter than usual at 122 cm / 4 ft, it took only 14 hours to make.

Flowing grids 2: on the diagonal

Whereas the previous process constructed the basic grid on a horizontal/vertical orientation, and then modified it to be diagonal, the next process constructs it on the diagonal.

It may be impossible to guess in advance what the results will be, but it can be fun finding out. This method was explored in the quest for grid movement like waves in the sea, but ended up in quite a different area.

To aid diagonal grid drawing, a basic diagonal skeleton of 10 cm squares was drawn up with 1 cm graduations, and card templates were drawn/cut around dinner plates and side plates. Two different grids were generated: gentle waves by the wide arc of the big plate and busier ones by the tighter arc of the smaller plate. The former, when crossed with itself, gave a viable grid (Figs 3.43 and 3.45); but the latter did not and had to be crossed with a straight grid (Fig 3.44). The results were surprisingly sexy, womanly curves (Fig 3.46).

The one that was made into lace as

Hot Spots also turned out to have 'hit the spot' more accurately than I could ever have imagined. A doctor who saw it being completed revealed that radiotherapy uses the principle that trajectories may be crossed within the body to focus on a deep-seated tumour; the target is known as the 'hot spot'. The colours in this body-shaped piece of lace had done exactly the same.

The other grid has tantalising possibilities but potentially unstable grids need to be used with strong, stable thread, or they may distort. A section of *Marcel* (Fig 3.39), made in nylon fishing line, twisted as soon as the pins came out, turning three times over a 2 m / 6 ft length. Accidental discoveries like this need to be exploited rather than resisted, but may take a while to resolve. It has been found that filaments made from resistant materials such as metal and plastic transmit twist instead of absorbing it, whereas fibres such as linen absorb twist better. Copper wire may be hammered back to shape, but thread wired with steel may have too much memory to be controlled in this way. Dismembered multi-core computer cable works well on bobbins.

Fig 3.43 *Bottom left: Curves crossed with curves and gridded Diagonal skeleton (purple) Gentle arc (green) Join corners (red) for grid*

Fig 3.44 *Bottom centre: Curves crossed with straight lines and gridded*

Fig 3.45 *Below: Dinner-plate grid*

Fig 3.46 *Inset: Hot Spots, 1993 Linen 16/2 95 x 38 cm*

Fig 3.47 *Main photo: Marcel Twist, 1999 Nylon monofilament 183 x 10 cm*

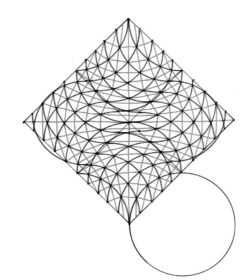

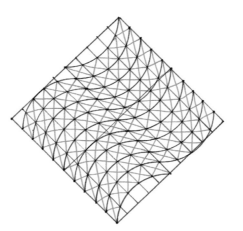

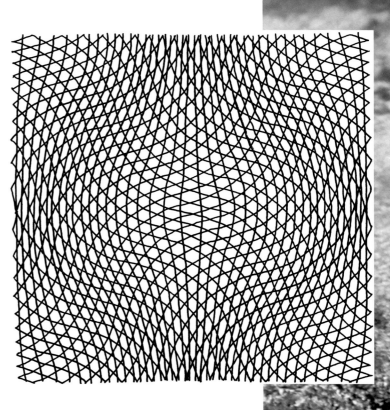

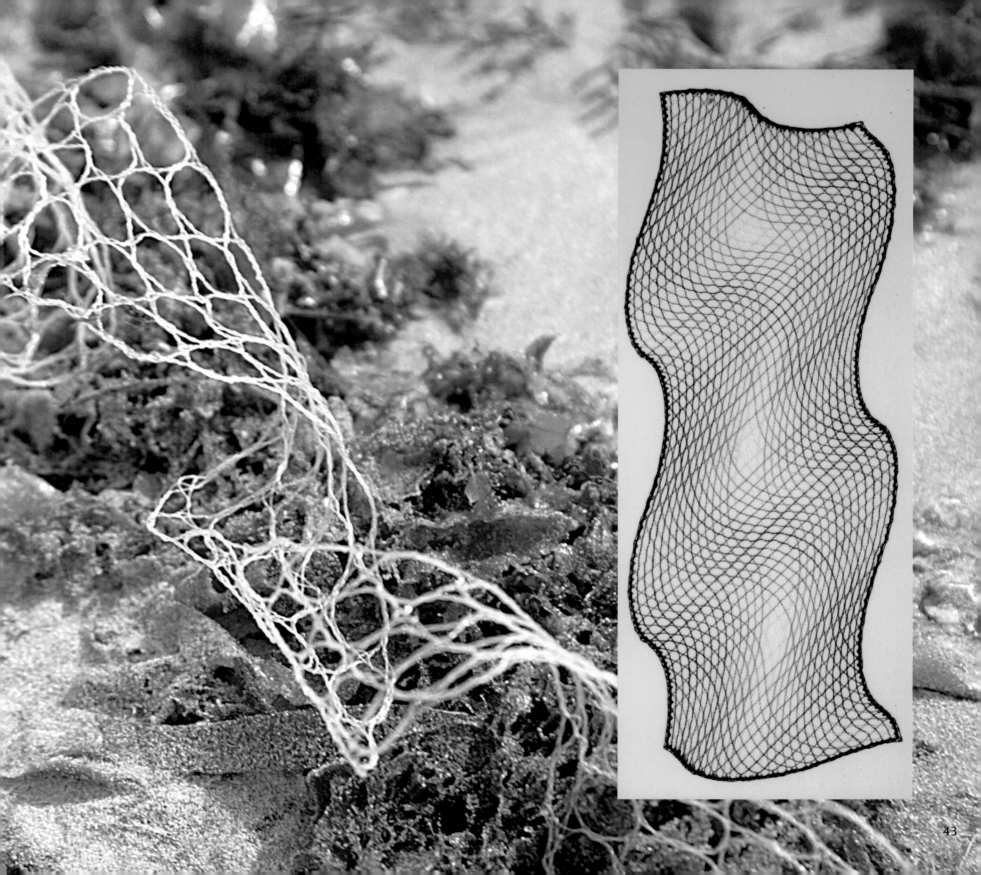

Allowing a design to evolve

A flowing grid can add a whole new aspect to a static design. The grid for the Ogee pattern was built up from the basic template in Fig 3.48, with guidelines drawn along the edge of each repeat to help orientate the design work (Fig 3.49).

The original intention was to create a scarf to go with a new coat (Fig 3.50) but as each sample was made, new possibilities kept opening up. A flowing grid drawn to exploit these then offered potential for a new series of designs.

The coat, printed using natural rust dyes, suggested a black lattice background which would allow russet threads to work through as diamonds. The first idea (Fig 3.51) then led to two more (Figs 3.52 and 3.53) with the lattice at first embellished and then separated.

Exploration opened up possibilities with subtlety as well as contrast, first using closely-allied colour values (Fig 3.53) and then exploring the more dramatic effect from dark, medium and light threads

as in Fig 3.54. It was at this point that speculation began on how this might develop on a curved grid (Figs 3.48 and 3.49). The mechanics of this grid followed the example on the previous page but an ellipse template was used instead of a circle in order to squash the shape into an 'ogee'.

Since the grid had one more dot per repeat than was needed for the pattern, the motifs were separated by a doubled-linen 'gimp' grid. Further explorations of the basic flowing grid followed, including honeycomb (Fig 3.55) and the deployment of revolving motifs inspired by Japanese design (Fig 3.56).

Since the grid is based on a square, straight edges are always available across the centre of each motif. The curved structure can be delicate, and may be inclined to straighten under heavy-handed laundering, but if the lace is wrapped around a short length of drainpipe or a lemonade bottle before washing, in the manner recommended for old lace, this is no longer a problem.

Fig 3.48 *Below:*
Pattern template from
ellipse stencil

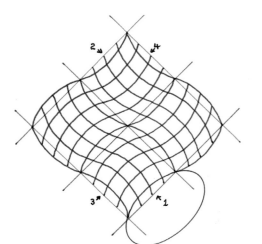

Fig 3.49 *Below:*
Ogee grid with
guidelines

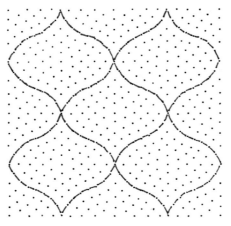

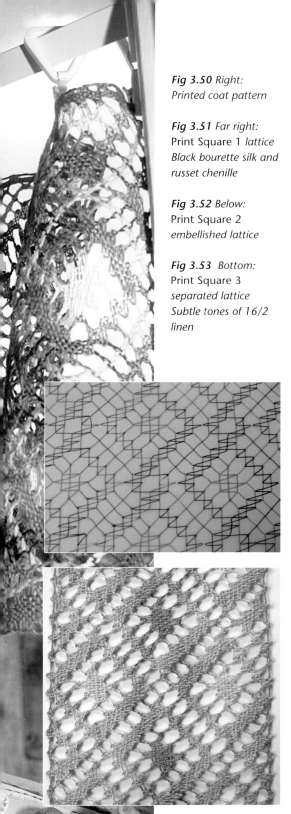

Fig 3.50 *Right:*
Printed coat pattern

Fig 3.51 *Far right:*
Print Square 1 *lattice*
Black bourette silk and
russet chenille

Fig 3.52 *Below:*
Print Square 2
embellished lattice

Fig 3.53 *Bottom:*
Print Square 3
separated lattice
Subtle tones of 16/2
linen

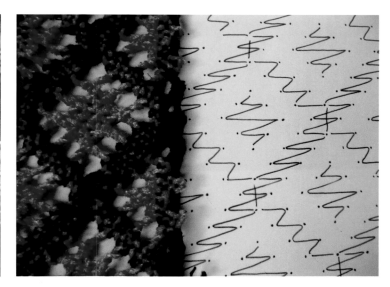

Fig 3.54 *Main photo,*
left:
Print Square Ogee
Café Curtain, *2010*
Linen 16/2 and
doubled 16/1
22 x 107 cm

Fig 3.55 *Below:*
Honeycomb Ogee
Grid *sample, 50/3 linen*

Fig 3.56 *Right:*
Woven Wave *sample*
Doubled 16/2 linen

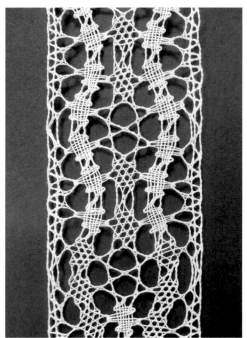

Expressive grids 1: nature

To find an irregular grid that fits the unique spirit of a natural phenomenon like swirling water or wave movement trapped in ice (Fig 3.59), we must fit the grid to the subject. This may be achieved by drawing a diagonal grid so that it deviates along and around the subject. Taking a simple example:

1 Draw a box around the subject, and mark equal graduations along all edges (Fig 3.57a). Mark these in a size that suits the thread you would like to use, say 1 cm for 16/2 linen (see page 135), to be assured that the grid will be suitable.

2 On a sheet of tracing paper and from the top left, number the graduations along the top and down the right side, and again down the left side and along the bottom.

3 Draw each diagonal line to end at the same number but allow it to accommodate to the subject as evenly as possible.

4 If you repeat this process in the opposite direction, on another layer and numbered from the opposite corner, you have not only a grid that suits this subject but one with other uses (b).

This was the process that revealed the sea movement being sought when *Hot Spots* came about. A previous pattern had examined air bubbles frozen in marsh ice on an ebbing tide, which had actually captured wave movement without my realising this (Fig 3.58). Exploration in colour showed that removing the outer sections left the ebb and flow effect (Fig 3.60) on which spume could be plotted for wave movement (Fig 3.62). This is another example where keeping the original grid underneath aids design and interpretation.

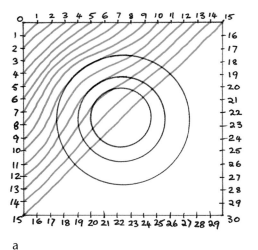

a

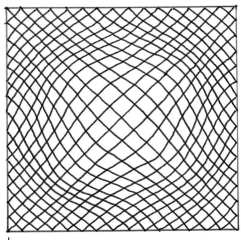

b

Fig 3.57 Above, left and right: *Expressive grid (a) in progress, (b) completed*

Fig 3.58 Right: Ice Flow, *1992 Linen 16/2 57 x 40 cm*

Fig 3.59 Below: *Inspiration for* Ice Flow

Fig 3.60 Right: Ice Flow *grid explored*

Fig 3.61 Below right: *Waves on the shore*

Fig 3.62 Main photo: Sea Foam, *1993 Linen, cotton, chenille, metallic 116 x 34 cm*

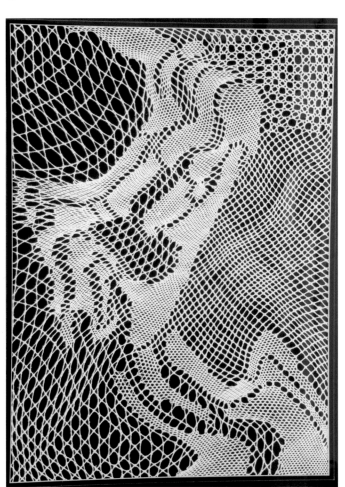

Expressive grids 2: emotive

Sometimes all that is necessary is a good idea and some freehand drawing, either vertical, horizontal or diagonal, to produce a grid with many uses.

Pitching oneself against problems set for other media can be enlightening. The grids on this page came out of an Open College of the Arts exercise aimed at general textile interpretation (but not lace) with a suggested size of 20 cm square and a time limit of two hours. This size and speed being a tall order for lace, the exercise marked an important step forward once it was resolved.

The aim of the course challenge was to interpret moods or themes. Any two could be selected from the list: *delicate, sensuous, rugged, tranquil, agitated, repulsive, shimmering, witty, restrained.*

Initial pieces stalled because they were made at a scale too large for the flimsy lace threads available.

I then bought thicker embroidery threads and started drawing grids that suggested the different moods. Each of these was made up with a suitable interpretation, for example the 'shimmering' theme was implemented with sparkling threads (Fig 3.63).

Of the original list, only 'repulsive' escaped because of time pressure, although my ideas had got as far as a construction that could be melted, dripped or rotted! The agate slice (Fig 3.64) turns from a tape into a square grid.

But never one to let a good grid go to waste when such an exercise is over, the *Butterfly Fish* tablemats (Fig 3.66) grew from the 'agitated' grid (Fig 3.65) to suggest the rippling of the water through which fish would move. Quick and simple to make, the final threads were knotted and left to form the tail fins, and the same colours were hung in at different places each time to vary the cloth stitch stripes.

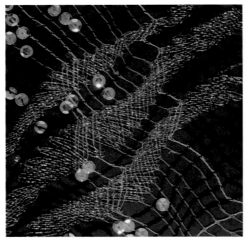
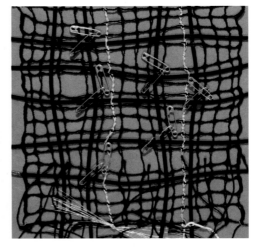

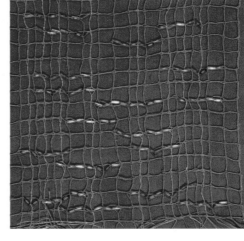
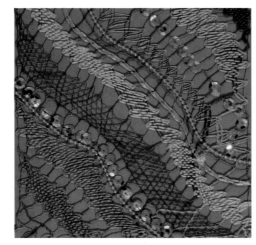
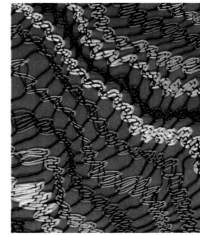

Fig 3.63 *Left, clockwise from top left: Shimmering, witty (punk – leather and safety pins), tranquil, agitated, sensuous, rugged, 1991 Each 20 x 20 cm*

Fig 3.64 *Bottom right:* Delicate 2, Agate slice, *1991 Linen, cotton, metallic 26 x 35 cm*

Fig 3.65 *Far right: Agitated grid*

Fig 3.66 *Main photo:* Butterfly Fish tablemats, *1992 Linen 16/2 13, 31 and 42 cm long First pub:* Lace Express

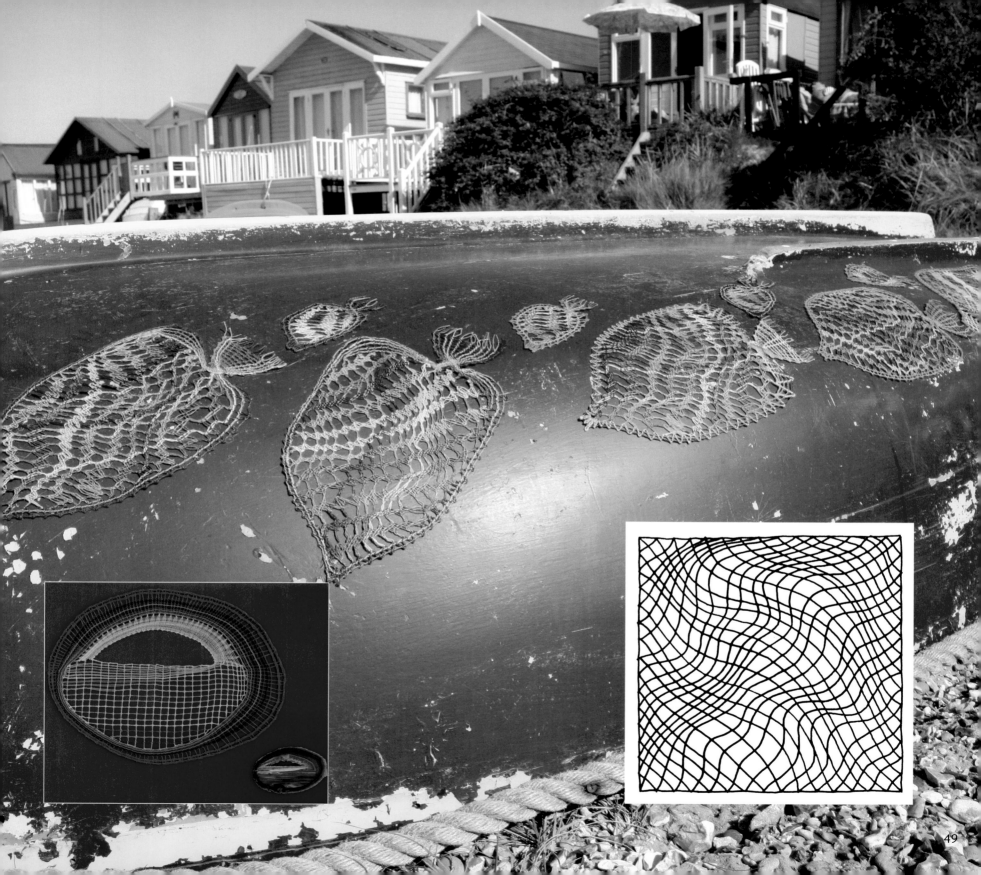

Mixing grids

Taking risks is part of moving forward, since we can often learn just as much by evaluating failure as from easily achieved success. The problems exposed may take time to rectify, but staying in one's comfort zone would eventually impede progress.

The threads I chose for the *Lace Cap* panel were the main risk, since I designed on a large scale for a mixture of threads, some of which were likely to be unstable. The design evolved over time around other work. Remaking with the benefit of hindsight is a serious option that should never be rejected.

A lace cap hydrangea in the garden presented an annual challenge: to draw, to record in colour, and to capture as a design in proportion to its vigorous personality. The flowers are a subtle mixture of pink, blue and mauve, stiffly presented on the bush, and the flowing, glossy-green leaves add a different character. It is not a sophisticated or rare plant; it is a blowsy old friend which repays pruning with abundance. So it was felt that interpretation needed to be in similar vein, but its size and the variety of its component parts represented a severe challenge to my artistic ability.

Dissatisfaction with pastel (Fig 3.69), crayon and photography (Fig 3.70) eventually led to drawing the outline of the image using the 'see-through pane' approach.

Set up at a suitable distance from the subject on a tapestry frame, a drawing was made on a sheet of clear plastic using coloured OHP pens. This approach is similar to that used by some Old Masters, who used soap on gridded glass, as well as lenses (see page 120).

The plastic was then covered in tracing paper and the drawing copied in ink. The flower and leaf motifs were photocopied and enlarged as a kit (Fig 3.68), cut out

and grouped as required. A grid matrix was drawn in the same way as for expressive grids (see Fig 3.57), but the flowers were gridded with straight lines, and the leaves and ground with expressive ones, joined at the edges of the petals.

Interpretation was with threads shaded along the top from pink at the centre through mauve to blue and green at the edges. The central parts of the flowers were made in plates of half-stitch, which mixed up the threads. For the whole-stitch florets, the first two threads that came up in the pink, blue or mauve group were used to make the petals, and

Fig 3.67 *Far left:*
Lace Cap, *1996*
Linen Tow 4, pearl 5
embroidery and DK
knitting cotton
111 x 39 cm

Fig 3.68 *Above left:*
Flowers from the kit

for the leaves it was the first two greens (with just two extra threads added when these proved insufficient).

The intention was to capture the bush in an impressionistic manner. Constructed on 1.5 cm grid, the finished piece had to be stretched and stapled onto covered board with the frame made round it. A more stable alternative would be to make the entire panel in shades of green linen, adding and subtracting the flower colours (as with *Wisteria*, page 100). Blocking the panel (page 130) could also have stabilised it.

Working lace bigger increases its impact, reduces the time to make

and therefore the cost. Since this size presented problems, the work that followed this project was reduced in size to fit thinner and more stable thread, while design was developed further. The discovery of stable threads for larger work, together with improved design, eventually allowed a return to a wider grid, which is more economical for commission work.

Unusual grids were explored as a way of presenting Torchon in a more personal manner. They have wide potential for development in other ways which are individual to you.

Fig 3.69 *Above left:*
Pastel studies for the
project

Fig 3.70 *Above:*
Composite photo

Fabulous Fibres

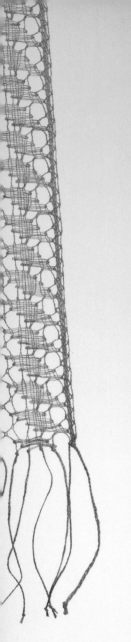

Getting to know your yarns

There are two routes to greater impact in modern lace; one is through design, and the other is through the filaments or fibres (threads or yarns) used.

If we allow the thicker and more interesting yarns to do the talking, design may be simplified, production time shortened and the lace given strong personality (Figs 4.1, 4.2).

Knowledge of properties of threads and yarns gives us personal control over our projects and allows us to calculate for the risks involved in using new yarns. Projects made from well-known threads might seem safer but may lack the thrill that awaits when a speculative use brings out unforeseen effects.

Many more yarns or threads are suitable for bobbin lace than might be expected:

- Fine threads may be plied and mixed to make up thicker ones.
- Embroidery, weaving and knitting yarns of all kinds may be incorporated, although some may need extra care.
- Tough and resilient yarns can add support to weak or fancy ones.
- Textured yarns can add tactile qualities to larger-scale lacemaking.
- Similar fibres may turn out to have been spun with different properties for different uses.

Beautiful fibres may also be spun by hand, leading to unique work impossible with commercial yarn.

We need to be able to discover the qualities that new yarns can add to lacemaking – such as colour, drape, sheen, softness or sculptural abilities – if we are to use each to its best advantage. 'Only the most intimate familiarity with materials can lead to the "feel" for their needs and their limits', wrote Ernst Gombrich in examining how crafts can thrive.[6]

The characteristics of each yarn may be discovered by making a sample piece of lace designed to evaluate its common and its unique properties. Making a sample (which may only take an evening – see page 62) will reveal:

- how suitable a yarn is for bobbin lace
- which size grid fits it
- how it handles on bobbins
- what the finished lace will be like
- how suitable the yarn is for working with a flexible grid
- if there are any problems to overcome
- any other surprising revelations.

A sample is also a safe place to practise finishing methods such as mangling and blocking (see page 130).

Some yarns come in a good range of fast-dyed colours. Others are only available in white and natural colours, which could be dyed at home; best for this are cotton, linen, silk and viscose rayon. Dyeing is a skill well worth acquiring (see page 65).

In the same way that top chefs use only quality ingredients, contemporary lace deserves the use of the best yarns. To take advantage of the broadest range, these may need to be ordered from specialist, international or commercial suppliers.

Many of the characteristics of available yarns have been evaluated and are shown in the tables on pages 134–37. This can be a good starting point, but there are still many good reasons to handle each yarn for ourselves and become better acquainted with it. And while we are getting to know the yarn, our mind may start to envisage the possibilities it offers.

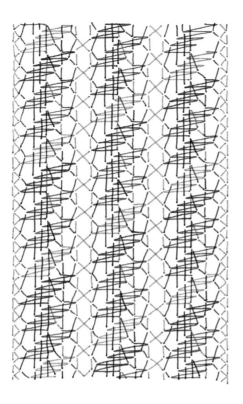

Fig 4.1 Left: Polka, 2007 *Rough Czech hemp dancing through smooth Polish linen 150 x 18 cm (excl. fringe) Simple and subtle results enabled by thread and design experimentation to demonstrate that less can be more; scarf intended to be sculptural rather than soft and pliable*

Fig 4.2 Above: *Thread diagram showing how to calculate where to hang in the rough thread (or create a colour scheme)*

Fig 4.3 Left:
Compuswirl II, 1997
*Anchor linen in three
natural shades
39 cm diameter
Thread available only
for a limited time in
the UK as few
bought it*

Fig 4.4 Above:
Pinebark 1, 2010
*Linen 16/2
148 x 16 cm
Scarf made to match
skirt*

Linen and cotton

Linen is strong, durable, lustrous and crisp – and can be expensive. It fell out of favour during the 'easy-care' boom but is a sustainable fibre of great character. It is the perfect fibre for lace, retaining its shape when tension is released. It comes in all sizes, from thick rug warp to fine weaving thread via all manner of yarns with really practical uses.

Its texture – smoothness softened by the occasional slub – may not suit everyone, but different processes can render it soft, stiff, smooth, rough and with variable qualities of drape. It can be made the main feature of a piece (Fig 4.3), or buried to support other yarns.

For instance, a scarf in which half of the threads are linen and the other half highly textured, will *look* textured but retain much of the stability of the linen (as in *Snow Leopard*, page 84). This might seem to add expense and inconvenience to a project but quality materials lead to durable lace.

Lace linen is spun in a wide range of colours, but availability can be a problem. However, sources are available in Continental Europe.

A reliable alternative is **weaving linen** (see Fig 7.4 page 88, and Fig 4.4); weight for weight it may be one-tenth of the price of lace linen, although it must be purchased in larger packages. The yarn tables on pages 134–37 show equivalent counts and the individual qualities of each linen, together with hints on avoiding problems.

Firms that recirculate yarn from various branches of the textile industry are goldmines for the experimental lacemaker. These yarns may not remain in circulation for very long and continuously stocked lines may change, perhaps in colour or texture, according to what is available. Sampling will reveal the true potential of the various yarns on offer, some of which provide good colour ranges.

Natural linen varies in colour (from grey to gold) and quality, according to source and processing. Some may look unremarkable but turn out to have very special qualities. Dyeing needs heat.

Linen is resilient, and may be rolled, posted or stored without problems. If it is mixed with steel, one cannot take such liberties, for steel has memory and will prevent the linen from returning to its original shape.

Cotton is cheap and ubiquitous. This is another fibre that changes its character according to the wide variety of ways it is processed.

Some embroidery yarns with a 'pearly' appearance can shine like silk, while some are matt. Cotton is strong and reliable, perhaps not as dramatic as linen or silk, but always useful. It dyes easily.

Weaving cotton (which can again be a fraction of the price of hobby yarn) can be a superior alternative to that produced for crochet and tatting. This yarn beds down well into cloth stitch.

There has been controversy in the textile community over the destructive practices which have ruined the land on which cotton is grown in some parts of the world. Ecologically sound cotton is now becoming easier to find.

*Fig 4.5 Main photo:
Sycamore scarf, 2003
Spun silk 8/2
150 x 24 cm
This has been
'finished' (see page
130)*

*Fig 4.6 Below:
Sample including
hand-spun bamboo
spun by Louise Taylor
(the lustrous thicker
thread) with silk, silk
chenille and linen*

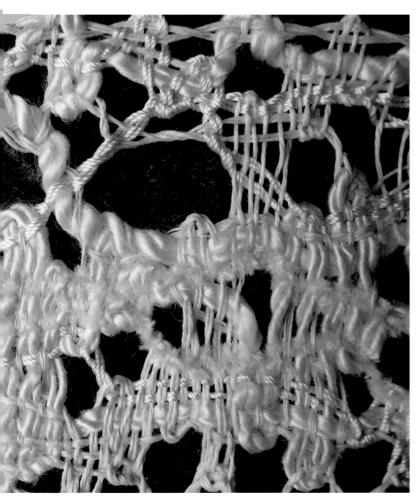

Silk, rayon and other fibres

Silk varies in sheen with the way it is produced and processed. When **filament silk** is lightly 'thrown' (twisted) into floss, its sheen is incomparable; the more it is twisted, the less it may shine. The shorter lengths of silk in **spun silk** take on a pearly lustre but polish up well once a garment has been 'finished' (Fig 4.5). **Bourette** is a highly textured silk which is obtained from cocoons where the moth has eaten its way out, causing damage that necessitates special processing to recover the silk.

Whether produced for weaving, embroidery or for knitting, silk will make a project special because of its lustre. It may be more costly than other fibres, but silk is strong, resilient, soft, warm and drapes beautifully – why make a scarf in lesser fibres when you can make it in silk?

Silk readily absorbs dye. Thick, commercially dyed silk is hard to find and dyeing it yourself a more economic option.

There is knitting silk which is lightly woven into a narrow tape, and low-twist filament silk, which plies beautifully. Both have great potential for extra development.

Viscose rayon varies in quality according to how it is processed, and should be selected carefully. Sampling really pays off here, exposing poor-quality thread, despite perhaps an attractive dye. Choose from a reliable make or supplier, and test all for strength, especially old fibre.

Rayon may be 'lively' to handle but it can add incomparable sheen and brilliant colour to a project at relatively low cost. Although a less expensive way of making something that looks very similar to silk, it deserves to be appreciated for its own qualities. Rayon is easy to dye at home.

Hemp is one of those fibres with the more eco-friendly credentials that are becoming popular as sustainability starts to take centre-stage. It is strong and pliant but with a fairly rough texture. It can be purchased in an interesting range of subtly coordinated colours that beg to be used in the right project – perhaps in large hangings where its texture can be put to good advantage.

Nettle, ramie, bamboo and banana offer unusual properties and textures which vary according to the way they have been processed. Nettle may have

the texture of sandpaper; ramie may sometimes look like linen, but may also be stiff and wiry. Among an ever-widening range of fibres available for hand-spinning, bamboo (Fig 4.6), banana and soya are soft and lustrous, and Tencel (made from wood pulp) is linen-like. These are superb for lace.

Natural raffia only comes in short lengths and this imposes a limit on a project, which might be no larger than a bag, perhaps. But synthetic raffia, which comes by the cone and looks like audio tape, may be made into larger pieces of lace.

Bamboo tape may offer possibilities for extra-large-scale work achievable otherwise only by wire. Dyed tape looks and acts very like raffia.

Knitting ribbons come in various fibres and dyes, and can be used alone or mixed with other yarns.

Knitting metallics may produce poor lace on their own, but shine when supported by wire. Some metallics can be problematic, yet some are highly reliable. Make samples to ascertain whether their qualities suit you. Metallics may be incompatible with other yarns because of different shrinkage rates.

Effect yarns such as fuzzy, paper-tied, slub, bouclé, chenille, eyelash, cord, and many other knitting and weaving yarns, can be given extra strength by incorporating reliable fibres like linen and cotton. Their use adds textural fun to lace projects. They do not have to be used in pairs; try a fine strong yarn with a fancy one, to reduce bulk.

Hand-spun yarn needs to be strong, resilient and not too hairy. It is best spun 2- or 3-ply or Navaho ply.

Working with wool and animal fibres

Wool is naturally springy and resilient, qualities which can work against the tension under which lace is made. However, some wool is spun to be stable, such as carpet, weaving and crewel wool, and it may also be hand-spun to give precisely the qualities sought by the lacemaker. Wool items may also be blocked (see page 130) to stretch them to their full beauty.

Certain animal fibres offer special qualities which may work well with the lace process – lustrous worsted-spun long-staple wool from Wensleydale sheep produces stable yarn and handspun kid mohair has a special sheen without the excessively hairy structure that can tangle on bobbins wound with adult mohair.

Among the many interesting commercial wools available, certain brands offer the lacemaker extra benefits. Noro yarn, produced in Japan with a high degree of hand-input, comes closest to hand-spun with beautifully blended products in luscious colourways. These may often be pulled straight from the ball to give interesting colour effects, especially for tape lace. Wool and wool blends with silk and cashmere may be single-ply, but if care is taken to retwist as soon as the yarn starts to unravel, breakages can be avoided. Thicker yarns may be used as passives with finer qualities, or linens, used as workers (Fig 4.7).

Hand-spun yarn for lace needs to be well-spun but not over-spun, two-, three- or four-ply, or Navaho ply, and a wide range of vegetable fibres such as flax, soya, tencel, bamboo and others may be incorporated.

The spinner who can make lace has a wide field open to her. Margaret Eaglestone chose to spin five colours – white Corriedale, grey Suffolk, light brown Border/Leicester, medium brown Shetland and chocolate Corriedale – from which she blended 15 colours to create the effect and colour of bark. Spinning an hour a day, the process including plying, washing and skeining took four months; the lacemaking was considerably swifter, the only problem being that the yarn needed constantly to be re-twisted.

Ann Allison, who farms in Yorkshire, had already tussled with a knitting yarn so springy 'it was like working with elastic', so chose Wensleydale for its stability, knowing it would not stretch or untwist easily but would also look good. She had the pattern reversed by computer to allow both ends to match.

Expensive fibres may be mixed with others to spread their qualities through a project more economically. Sampling a small ball of cashmere showed the yarn to be strong and stable, yet extremely soft; the yarn that was left was then used to fill half the bobbins needed for a scarf, with the others wound with silk and linen to enhance the cashmere colour. The lace (Fig 4.8) has the soft and stable quality of the cashmere, added to the lustre of silk and extra personality from the linen, so that it is not as limp as a 100% cashmere scarf might be.

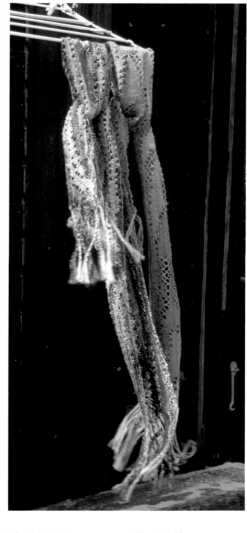

Fig 4.7 *Main photo:*
Lace for Spinners,
2003
Simple tape-lace
scarves using minimal
technique
Purple scarf:
Noro Iro wool/silk
passives with Cash
Iroha lambswool/
cashmere passives
155 x 25 cm

Pink scarf:
Noro Kureyon
wool passives with
Vuorelman 4 linen
tow workers and some
passives
152 x 24 cm

Fig 4.8 *Inset:*
Pinebark 7, *2010*
Patricia Roberts
cashmere, with
Zurcher tussah silk and
Bockens 16/2 linen
wound together on
other bobbins
128 x 12 cm

Fig 4.9 *Above:*
Woodgrain *wool*
scarves
Ann Allison, 2003
Wensleydale, crewel
and acrylic yarns
162 x 22 cm
Margaret Eaglestone,
2009
Handspun plied
natural-coloured
fleeces
154 x 18 cm

Mixing threads and avoiding problems

Without realising it, lacemakers may well already have drawers full of threads that can be used in larger-scale work – embroidery threads of all sizes may be blended just by winding several harmonious ones onto a bobbin at once. Colour schemes, both subtle and bright, can be greatly enhanced when suitable threads are plied together. This may entail mixing fibres, but knitting yarn manufacturers have been doing that for years. By looking at the way they enhance fancy threads with plain ones, carrying special effects along with stable fibres that make the bulk of the garment, we can easily do the same thing ourselves.

There are various ways in which thread mixing may enhance lace:

- Creating a subtle undertone by adding one fine thread in a special colour to each yarn selected for a project (Fig 4.10).
- Blending yarns of one fibre, say silk, from our store of embroidery threads. A variety of thicknesses and colours may be plied into one desired weight to create many related shades (Figs 4.11, 4.12).
- Examining the material in a favourite garment for all the colours in it, and then creating yarns to match – perhaps in various weights (Fig 4.13).

A glint of metallic may be added, perhaps with one or two fine threads to enhance the whole. Lacemakers have always been cautious about mixing threads in different fibres because of different shrinkage rates, but it seems worth taking this risk in order to create attractive pieces.

Fine, soft yarns may strengthen when plied, and some fascinating ones like silk/steel or linen/steel may be plied to give greater versatility.

Aim to make the created yarns of similar thickness to each other, and always make a sample before you start work in earnest, to make sure the pattern is the right size.

A stock of good-quality yarn is like a kitchen larder: a collection of ingredients that may be used in different combinations for a variety of delicious creations into the future. It is vital to be able to rely on repeatable yarns and some used in this book have remained in production for many decades. Work would therefore be easy to replicate for commission.

Poor-quality yarn may actually deteriorate; brittle yarn knotted under tension around the top bar of a hanging was found to have snapped after ten years in storage. This suggests that all hangings should be self-contained, and should be sewn onto hanging bars with strong thread.

Fig 4.10 Inset: Sample with aqua undertones, constrasting with cool greys in the other sample

Fig 4.11 Main photo: Brick scarf, 2009 Silks including dyed spun silk, Tussah 2/20, Gütermann S300, Vineyard Silk, Texere Roma and Dynasty, plied and mixed to an even weight 149 x 11 cm

Fig 4.12 Above: Shades created from plied silks

Fig 4.13 Left: Pink samples, thick and thin

Sampling and 'Texing'

Making samples allows us to be self-sufficient when it comes to yarn choice. It can give confidence in the handling of existing yarns, and new ones may be tested to ascertain their capabilities. Sampling exposes the yarn's limpness, stiffness, handling qualities, strength or weakness, general character, and tendency to unravel or pull apart.

Making up a sample is a simple way to fit any yarn to its correct grid size. To do this, a pattern designed to accommodate a range of increasing dot-pitches is needed, which may be found on page 138. Making up the sample will show exactly which grid results in the density of cloth stitch that is desired in the lace.

To determine the starting point, it may be appropriate to compare the yarn to be tested with one of known characteristics and to use its recommended dot-pitch. One way of doing this is to find a known yarn with a similar Tex number; this may mean having first to Tex your new yarn. Tex is a way of comparing yarns according to their linear density. Wool, cotton and silk all use completely different 'count' systems but the Tex count is an international standard based on the weight in grams of one kilometre of any yarn.

We can use the Tex count to determine which yarns will match a preferred grid size. The yarn tables on pages 134–37 show my Tex counts for many different types of yarn, together with an idea of a suitable dot-pitch.

Unhelpfully, most yarns sold have no indication of their Tex count. Some yarns, such as Vuorelman of Finland, do have a published Tex count, but this is unusual.

Fortunately, it is easy to calculate the Tex count for ourselves. We just need to measure out a 10 metre length of yarn, weigh it on scales sensitive to 0.1 gram

(such as the Salter 1250) and multiply the result by 100. This gives the Tex number. A metre-measure can be created by fixing two nails, 1 metre apart, into a piece of wood. Winding on five loops of yarn will give the required 10 metre length. This method was devised by Peter and Jaquie Teal, and most of the yarns in the yarn table have been 'Texed' in this way.

Of course, even yarns of the same Tex may have widely different characteristics when used in lace, but these will start to become apparent as we proceed with a sample.

To use the sample pattern:

1 Wind 14 pairs; one arm's-length for fine yarns/small samples, two for thicker/larger ones.
2 Set up pins at a dot-pitch that you think might be suitable for your yarn.
3 Make up the first diamond. If this appears to be too loose (or you think it could take being tighter), unpick and move it to a closer pitch grid. It is good to know the minimum pitch possible for log or curved grids.
4 Now make up the full sample, with whole and half-stitch diamonds, through the range of increasing dot-pitches until the lace appears unviable. (This will be a matter of judgement that will be confirmed after taking the lace off the pillow.) Note that some yarns still make reasonable lace much further on than might be expected, especially with extra twists in the ground.
5 Knot off, remove the pins and examine the sample, holding it up to the light to decide which dot-pitch gives the best whole-stitch coverage. Tie a swing ticket beside the best, writing the details and optimum grid for future reference. It is also good to confer with friends.

If, after making the sample, the lace twists, snags or distorts, make a note for future reference. Similarly, record if the thread frays, gets tangled on the bobbin, parts in use or snaps at the knot. Tendencies to unravel or pull apart may be counteracted by re-twisting the yarn. This information will help to decide whether the yarn is worth extra care in handling, should it possess qualities that make this extra trouble worthwhile (Colcoton being a prime example of one that does).

Some yarns will surprise, and suggest new uses as we sample them; some may look similar to others but reveal unsuspected properties in use.

Fig 4.14 Below: *Sampling pattern*

Fig 4.15 Right: *Sampling and 'Texing'*

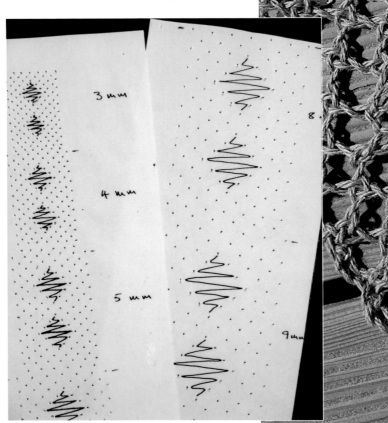

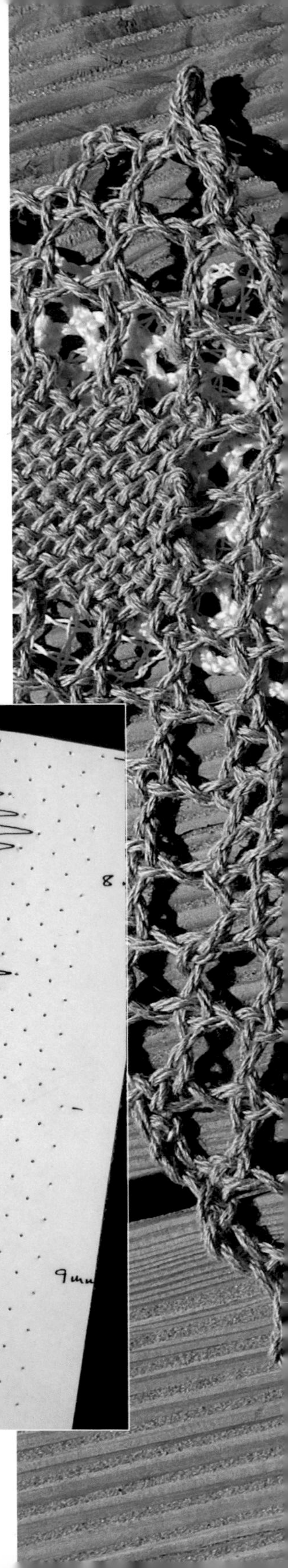

a good substitute for a 'swift') and tie it loosely with figure-of-eight ties in several places so it does not tangle. Fine threads may be wrapped around a short length of pipe. Wash the yarns first and dye them wet.

The methods described here are surprisingly easy to learn and apply, once we are properly organised and equipped. To avoid a messy kitchen, we can use Procion dyes in the garden or site a small boiler in the garage.

Procion dyes

Fibre-reactive dyes such as Kemtex Procion MX may be used on natural fibres such as cotton, silk, wool and viscose rayon (which is derived from wood pulp). Yarn can be dipped in dye solution and then left to soak in a plastic bag for a couple of hours, or even overnight. With just four basic dyes, an infinite number of colours can be achieved. They are fixed with solutions of washing soda and salt which can be added to the dye in one easy process.

The thread for the silk scarf shown opposite was dyed in buckets in a double-graduated dye system devised by the quilter Katy J. Widger.

1 Divide 1 litre of dye in half, and dilute one half with water to make it back up to 1 litre.
2 Take this new diluted litre and repeat the above process until there are five dye buckets graduating in strength.
3 Skein 35 hanks of yarn, dividing them into five piles of six, with five over.
4 Dye six hanks in each bucket and wash them.
5 Make up a second dye graduation that will mix well with the first. Retain one dyed hank from each of the first buckets and distribute the other hanks into each of the second buckets, adding an undyed hank to each.

This gave 35 related colours from the one dyeing process, and these were used for *Woodgrain* (Fig 4.16). Another version has been made by a spinner who spun and plied 15 different colours from five shades of natural fleece (see Fig 4.9, on page 59).

Indigo

Although indigo may be dyed in a bucket, it is hard to keep this at a steady temperature, so Burco boilers were used for my dyeing session. Different temperatures are needed for animal proteins (wool, silk) and cellulose fibres (cotton, linen, viscose). The dye liquor was prepared from synthetic indigo.

After being immersed for between five and fifteen minutes (longer for wool than cotton), the dyed fibres may be removed. These will be yellow, but quickly turn blue as the indigo magically oxidises in the air. For a deeper colour, re-dip for a few minutes. Leave it to air-dry for an hour or more. After rinsing in vinegar, washing in soap and rinsing, the process is over. Yarns must be left to dry out of bright sunlight, before balling (Fig 4.17; see the lace on page 93).

If you are apprehensive about dyeing your own yarn, there are many spinners, weavers and dyers who can help. Thankfully, I had the assistance of Jaquie Teal, who used a recipe from *A Handbook of Indigo Dyeing* by Vivien Prideaux, and quilter Mary Hewson who guided me through the graduated dyeing process. Further details of Procion dyeing may be found in *Dyeing in Plastic Bags* by Helen Deighan.

Fig 4.16 Left: Woodgrain *scarf, 1995* Texere spun silk 2.5/2, 5/2, 8/2, 16/2 *154 x 21 cm* Double-graduated dye, with successive colours planned into the lace by tracing thread paths

Fig 4.17 Above: Natural threads dyed with synthetic indigo

Dyeing your own threads 1: Chemical dyes

Commercial yarns have their limitations and some ambitious projects are only possible if you dye (or even spin) your own yarns. As someone who lives in jeans, I had long wanted to make indigo lace, but found few suitable yarns on sale. I also wanted to make heavy, coloured silk lace but found the ideal yarn had been discontinued.

Dyeing yarn for lace can follow the recipes for cloth, as long as we skein our yarns first (an extendable skirt hanger is

Dyeing your own threads 2: Natural indigo

'Indigo does not need heat if you use natural indigo,' Vivien Prideaux remarked when she saw the scarf I had made with the threads I had dyed with synthetic indigo. So she kindly offered me one of half-a-dozen bio-fermentation methods she had trialled in India in 2008/09 which may be used quite simply at home.

Vivien has used this method in cold weather, but I sited my vat in my greenhouse during the summer. All the utensils were cheaply obtained from surplus stores, with the lime – sold as 'hydrated' lime (not 'hydraulic', which is the wrong kind) – from a builder's merchants. The indigo is imported by Vivien from India in charcoal-like lumps and needs to be pulverised before use.

Take all precautions to protect yourself and your clothes (wear rubber gloves and do not inhale the finely-powdered lime), and do not re-use the utensils for food.

Vivien's book gives instructions for 'scouring' threads before dyeing to remove their dressing; cotton and linen threads should be boiled in water for 45 minutes with a tablespoon of washing soda, while silk can be soaked overnight in a soap solution.

Despite insufficient scouring, leaving lumps in the indigo and starting off with the wrong kind of lime, my vat did work when the problems had been resolved. The liquor should be the colour of French mustard when it is ready for dyeing.

Unlike with the synthetic indigo, where we immersed and left the yarns, with natural indigo you loop the wetted skein round your hands, lower it into the vat (without disturbing the lime at the bottom) and then take it straight out, manipulating it to make sure the air gets to all the threads and oxidises them, turning them blue.

The colour is built up by repeated dipping – a skein may be hung up for half-an-hour and then re-dipped. As the skeins slowly take deeper colour, this becomes addictive. The colour does dry much paler, and the process could take several days – the skeins shown here are only part-way through the process. They may be left for a week before washing through, to aid retention of the dye.

Vivien recommends that a short piece of yarn be retained from each dip, so you can record the colours obtained, and she suggests dyers keep copious notes. The vat can be kept going for a considerable time by stirring in the morning before use in the afternoon, or in the evening before dyeing next morning. Stir once a day if you are not using it.

Fig 4.18 Main photo: Lumps of natural indigo

Fig 4.19 Inset: Yarn dyed with natural indigo

Fig 4.20 Below left: Liquor ready to dye

Fig 4.21 Below right: 25 kg of hydrated lime

Fig 4.22 Bottom: Dyeing in progress

Preparation of 'India 4' vat

Equipment:
- 25-litre, smooth-bottomed plastic container with lid
- Strong, smooth stirring stick/ broom handle
- Stainless steel bowl, 1.5 litres
- Plastic container (e.g. ice-cream carton)
- Large plastic spoon
- Scales (500 g)

Ingredients:
- Slaked lime 580 g
- Soda ash (washing soda) 180 g
- Natural indigo 150 g
- Chopped dates 57 g

Method:
Day 1, morning: put 20 litres water in lidded container in a warm place. Afternoon: add
160 g slaked lime
60 g washing soda.
Stir with wooden stick.

Day 2: add
160 g slaked lime
60 g washing soda.
Stir as before.

Day 3: as Day 2

Day 4, morning: add
75 g powdered indigo, stir.
Evening: add
75 g powdered indigo, stir.

Day 5: mix 28 g slaked lime with 57 g chopped dates in 1 litre water, boil for 10/20 minutes. Add the mixture while hot to the vat and stir.

Day 6: the vat should be ready. If not and it has white foam, add 34 g washing soda; if too slimey, add 34 g dates, stir, leave for 24 hours.

5 Courage with Colour

A question of values

It might take quite a while to build up a stock of yarn in a broad range of colours but if we can make the colours that we do have work well together, we can make the most of a limited palette.

Of particular importance in lace, because of the way threads mix, is learning how to gauge the lightness and darkness of the colours we use. This is known as their value. Light threads can look out of place in the middle of dark ones, and vice versa.

Here is a little colour vocabulary to start with:

- A hue family (for example, green) contains many variations (sage green, apple green etc.).
- Primary colours are the pure hues of red, blue and yellow (see colour wheel, Fig 5.2).
- Secondary colours mix two primaries to make violet, green and orange.
- Complementary colours, found on the opposite sides of the colour wheel, harmonise with each other.
- Shades have added black.
- Tints have added white.
- Tones have added grey, or are a way of assessing the relative values of colours.
- Value is a measure of the quantity of light a colour reflects, which can be assessed on a graduated greyscale.
- Saturation is the depth or intensity of colour in a hue or mixture.

We may initially be concerned with hue, but each hue or colour reflects a different amount of light and will appear lighter or darker than others, which is its tonal value. We can use a tonal (grey) scale to assess this level of light, and compare this value with others, by using a shade strip (see Fig 5.4, or download from www.contemporarylace.com).

The tonal greyscale is evenly graded from light to dark, and to use it we punch a hole in the centre of each grey tone on the strip. We place each hole in turn over a reel of thread and watch for the point when the colour in the hole blends best with the grey value around it. Make a note of this value. If we group our threads by value, then colours will blend better. Sometimes similar tones of different colours look more harmonious than contrasting shades and tints of a single colour.

To group shades/tones/tints that have been wound onto bobbins, arrange them on the floor or table and squint down at them. This reduces the amount of colour the eye takes in and emphasises the tonal value. A 'ruby beholder' (Fig 5.3) may also help. This is a thick piece of red plastic often used by quilters, which reduces colour to tone. Then shuffle your bobbins about until each is in its correct tonal place – perhaps shading from one side to another, edge to middle, or whatever is your choice.

The advantage of doing this is that although the threads may mix in the lace, there is a good chance that the value groupings will remain near each other. Values can change their apparent quality of lightness and darkness according to the values that surround them, so time used for planning before lacemaking is well spent.

A good colour wheel from an art shop, or a book on colour for textiles, such as colorWorks by Deb Menz, can demonstrate colour harmonies (such as complementary, analogous, split-complementary, etc.) and explain how to operate value 'keys' to group closely related values.

Colour sample cards for thicker yarns can be tempting, although manufacturers seldom produce the wide variety of shade options available, for example in stranded cotton. Judging value as well as hue is an important part of knowing how to make the best use of those we select.

Fig 5.1 Main photo: Shade cards for weaving and embroidery in silk, linen, cotton and rayon

Fig 5.2 Inset: Colour wheel from colorWorks

Fig 5.3 Below left: Ruby beholder

Fig 5.4 Below: Shade strip with Bockens linen no.31

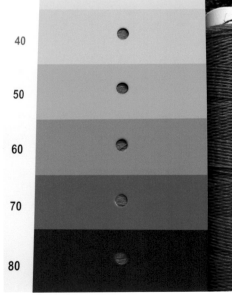

Judging colour transitions

Contrasting colours can be made to harmonise by introducing intermediary colours. For instance, orange and blue, being complementary colours, will intensify each other when placed side by side, but we can tone this down by adding blended colours in between. The paint strips at the bottom of the page include one showing mahogany colours that may be used (Fig 5.5).

Painters can easily mix one colour with another to produce a third, so paint exercises are a good place to develop the judgement needed to gauge colour transitions, before transferring that to yarn selection.

1 Draw ten 4 cm boxes on drawing paper.
2 Using an opaque medium such as gouache or acrylic, paint the first and last box in two different colours.
3 Then work from one colour to the other in even stages by mixing the two colours in different proportions.
4 Cut them out and arrange them in a graduated line.

We can try this with tints or tones of single colours, and learn even more by shading from a tint of one colour to the tone of a second. Exercises like these help

us develop an appreciation of the effect of colour transition and blending.

Yarn colours bought 'off the peg' seldom allow such subtle transitions but we can mix similar yarns from different manufacturers, or add different types of yarn which have the colours we are seeking, or blend the required colour from thinner threads.

We can also use combinations of yarns that come in two or more thicknesses (such as Bockens and Klippans linen, pearl cotton and William Hall super mercerised cottons), or as fine threads which may be plied (Texere Connemara). Stranded cotton often offers the precise shade needed, but is limited in length.

Once in control of our colour choices, we can operate 'painterly' effects, such as luminosity, where cleverly arranged colours seem to light each other up.

It is possible to achieve a luminous effect by:

■ surrounding a hue by darker values of the same colour
■ surrounding it by its complementary colour
■ outlining it in black or a dark colour
■ making it brighter than its surroundings
■ using a pure hue contrasted with a dull one.

Patterns that closely interweave threads (Figs 5.7, 5.8) are good places to observe the effects that colours have on each other. In Fig 5.6, the pink threads gain extra vibrancy from being juxtaposed with a darker maroon. A brilliant green adds to the optical mixture, an effect described later.

Practice makes perfect and it may take time and experience before the interaction of colours in our work becomes easy to handle. Once gained, this skill will permit a wide range of different threads to be used.

Fig 5.5 *Left: Painted colour strips*

Fig 5.6 *Right: Luminosity in action, paint and thread Detail from Monet's* Grainstack (Sunset) *Juxtaposition of harmonious threads in a* Paintworks *variation*

Fig 5.7 *Main photo:*
Paintwork *cushion,*
1999
Linen tow 4, knitting
and weaving cottons
and textures
42 x 40 cm
First pub: Lace Express

Fig 5.8 *Left:*
Leftover paint slicked
from the palette, taken
as the starting point
for Paintwork pattern

Optical mixing

When we look at colour, the eye eventually tires and produces an after-image in the complementary colour of the one in view. We can use this phenomenon to enhance our colour schemes in a process called 'optical mixing'.

In *The Principles of Harmony and Contrast of Colours*, M E Chevreul described this effect, which then inspired many of the experiments at the heart of Impressionism.

To understand how this process works, stare at the red square on this page (Fig 5.9) for about 30 seconds and then look at the white space beside it. You should see a green square.

Similarly, if we view two colours together, the after-image of one will be affected by the other. To see this at work, stare at the green square in the centre of the orange one (Fig 5.10) for 30 seconds. The green area should appear to be invaded by a greenish-blue aura, while the inner edge of the orange gains

a tinge of red. This is called 'simultaneous contrast'. Adding these 'perceived' colours into a green/orange colour scheme will automatically intensify the effect (Figs 5.11, 5.12).

It is worth taking the time to explore the effects of all the other primary and secondary colour combinations and to use the effects in our lace.

To enhance coloured threads, small amounts of complementary colour may be mixed on the bobbin or juxtaposed in the lace. Little flecks of green will intensify red, or flecks of red enhance green, just as Monet added poppies in a green field, or Van Gogh painted mauve shadows in a sweep of corn.

In the red scarf shown here (Fig 5.13), the passive threads were enhanced with green threads and slubs. Each pair is two individually created colour combinations knotted at the start. The effect of the scarf pattern is to group the passives vertically and alternate the workers (Fig 5.14). Both of these may be shaded and arranged in a variety of options.

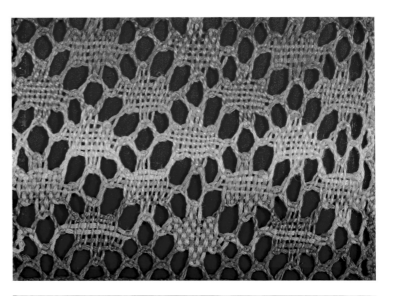

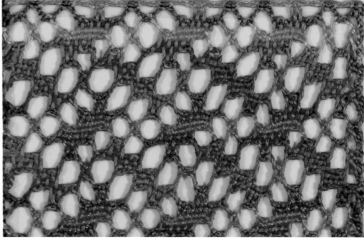

Fig 5.9 Below:
Red square in white
space

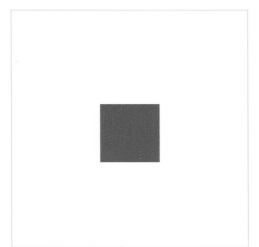

Fig 5.10 Below:
Orange square with
green in the middle

Fig 5.11 Top:
Orange shaded to
green through yellow;
relatively dull
11 x 9 cm

Fig 5.12 Above:
Orange and green
with bluish green;
more intense

Fig 5.13 Main photo:
Pinecone *scarf (red),*
1997
Linen tow 4 and
knitting cottons
180 x 20 cm
Paired but individually
created red passives
(enhanced with green
threads and slubs)
shaded across the
width of the scarf with
alternating textured

workers with Cone
variation (blue), 1998
Linen tow 4 and
textured knitting yarns
125 x 21 cm
Pattern effect
'tweaked' to allow
textured passives to
become workers

Fig 5.14 Inset:
Pinecone *scarf thread*
diagram

Colour control

Once we start adding a variety of colours to our lace, we become more aware of what happens to individual threads. In regular geometric patterns, thread paths repeat, allowing us to plan work that looks deceptively complex but may be easily made.

Our knowledge of how to follow or subvert thread paths will build with experience. For instance, the bobbins for the blue scarf on the previous page (Fig 5.13) were wound with many different textures but if you follow the pattern correctly only two worker pairs alternate in each column. This would not have taken advantage of the prepared textures. However, it proved fairly simple to switch pairs from passive to worker at the start of each motif, to allow all the textures a chance to become workers at some point or another. A design of this nature can be made in threads of all sizes. The finer the thread chosen, the smaller and more complex the pattern and the effects can become (Fig 5.16).

Simple diaper (small repeating) patterns of many kinds allow useful experimentation with colour control. A good way to start is with a pack of pens and some tracing paper, tracing thread paths to investigate how they run through a pattern, and how placing threads differently at the start can change the effects they produce.

Often there are more alternative interpretations in a simple pattern than we can imagine. A key manoeuvre in those explored here was to colour certain blocks as cloth stitch and then trace the colours back to the top of the pattern.

Making patterns in lace as well as working on paper helps to nurture our understanding of the process.

A small amount of design will go a long way. The examples shown here could make attractive scarves (see page 60) or could be developed into screens. Small experiments can be downloaded from www.contemporarylace.com to make colourful in-fills for the pockets of a Clippykit display bag.

Fig 5.15 *Main photo:*
Pinecone tablemats,
2000
Bockens linen 16/2
41 x 23 cm
First pub: Lace Express

Fig 5.16 *Right:*
Mary Pownall
Pinecone notebook,
2005
Pipers 3fold 90 silk
floss
16 x 10 cm

Fig 5.17 *Below:*
Three ways of
controlling colour
effects in one pattern

Fig 5.18 *Far right:*
Thread path sample,
1993
Linen 16/2

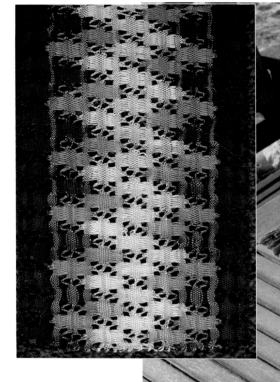

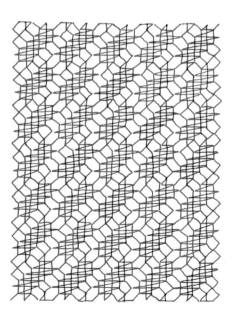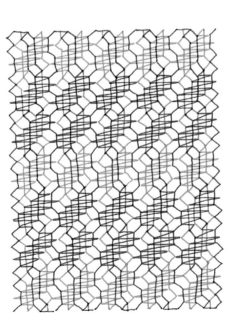

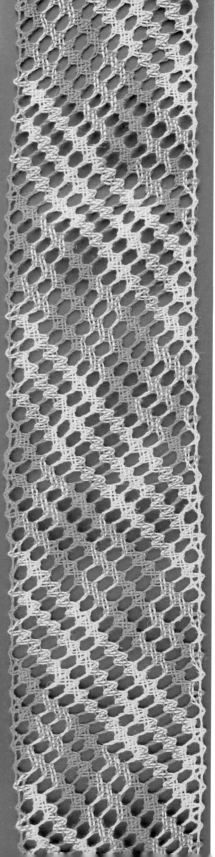

Controlling circles

Regular patterns can set up an internal dynamic which becomes interesting in itself. Once it is possible to calculate where threads will travel, we can plan colour schemes that deliver effective shading or the rhythmic repetition of colour.

The petals in *Waterlily* are packed so tightly together that the threads have nowhere to go, other than straight from one petal to the next as passives and in alternate blocks as workers. This was confirmed in coloured crayon before making. The diagram shown here demonstrates that the pattern may be shaded in six colours, while the sample shows that three would also be effective.

Drawing patterns up as diagrams is a useful way of recording thoughts and calculations if lacemaking time is short or the right threads for the project need to be researched.

Finding suitable thread in coordinated colours may be difficult. Those chosen for *Waterlily* in Colcoton were not perfect but the best that could be found at the time. This was an occasion where a graduated dye would have been particularly effective. Another option would have been to enlarge the pattern for thicker threads. Moravia linen could be used for three-colour versions, in 40/2 for A3 or 50/4 at A2 (141%). Since the threads are closely packed, tension must be excellent at the smaller size, but Moravia can also support a 110% enlargement.

To fill the hole in the middle, a separate roundel was made for the stamens. Polar patterns otherwise need mounting, best done in three-sided stitch (see Fig 10.1 page 124, *Influenced by Adam*) with the fabric then cut close to the stitching.

Some polar designs break easily into sections which allow the outer part to be made in a thicker count or a different colour from the inner section, as in Fig 10.1. This satisfactorily resolves the changes in dot-pitch. A further example of colour control in circles may be found on page 103.

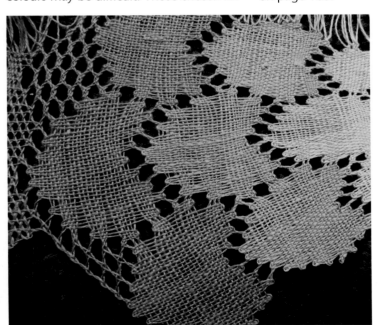

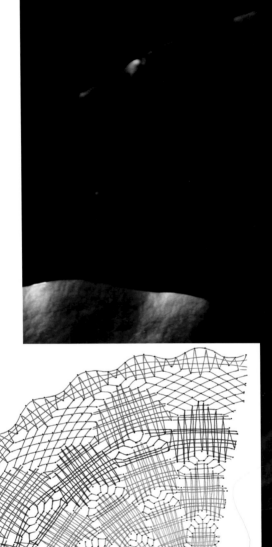

Fig 5.19 Left: Sample in three colours

Fig 5.20 Right: Thread diagram for six colours

Fig 5.21 Main photo: Waterlily, 2002 Colcoton 34/2 in six colours 26 cm diameter

Fig 5.22 Left:
Colour exploration
1987
From Mahonia leaf,
long faded, shown
with freshly cut leaves

Figs 5.23–5.25
Right, clockwise
from bottom:
Photograph, colour
study, lace sample
Nikki Nelson, 2006

Colour schemes

Translating the beauty of the environment into lace may take some time, during which visibility of the original stimulus cannot be guaranteed. We therefore need an effective way of recording the colours and colour combinations present in the subject, so that they will be to hand when we are ready to design and make our lace.

The method demonstrated here is a simple way of analysing and creating a permanent record of colour schemes that attract us. It works in many situations, from analysing a picture to examining a beautiful leaf, shell or pebble. It uses colour patches torn from glossy magazines such as *Vogue*, which have high-quality colour photography as well as printing. Pantone colour papers (expensive to buy), or paint-mix colour charts from a DIY store (often free), may also be used, with glue and scissors.

While the example shown here (Fig 5.22) has eight squares along each side (64 in all) the process will still be effective with a lower number, which is also quicker. Using this method encourages us to examine our inspiration more closely than usual, to take account of colour proportions and to look into shadows and textures.

Choose the subject you would like to translate into lace and closely observe all the colours within it. Then draw up a grid of 2 cm / 1 in. squares in the size you prefer. Fill each square with a separate colour, torn or cut from your magazine and colour sheets, to build up the grid so that it represents the subject as far as is possible. This will be similar in manner to a pixellated photo on the computer.

This will be a lasting reminder, portable enough to be carried around, as the search for threads of the right colours proceeds (Figs 5.23–5.25).

Control in chaos

The experiments in this book have been aimed at discovering quick and colourful ways to attract a new audience which may previously have closed its mind to other possibilities. Working with many colours at once also opens up the lace process to the experienced maker, revealing how threads work through patterns and allowing us to make new and improved versions.

In the sample shown here (Fig 5.26), green and blue floss silk was wound onto an equal number of bobbins and hung so that the greens went off in one direction and the blues in the other. The pattern, inspired by Peruvian weaving, allowed them to 'play' in what looked like a random manner, but where each colour became a worker, the resulting block was in a strong colour.

This discovery opened up wide possibilities but a fairly limited number of techniques have been found to deliver the best results. Most of the coloured abstract patterns shown in this book involve the use of whole-stitch trails and half-stitch ground.

- In whole-stitch trails, passive pairs descend vertically, whereas in half-stitch they split up in different directions.
- Half-stitch ground sends colours diagonally through the lace, while whole-stitch ground zigzags them vertically.
- Half-stitch ground also makes a more stable construction, although whole-stitch ground still produces beautiful, but different, lace.

Allowing coloured threads free rein, to go where they will, can present problems. Pale threads can look out of place in dark areas, for instance. Instead, a colour that looks as if it might stray too far may be

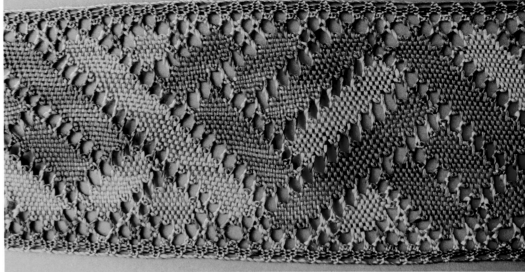

Fig 5.26 Right:
Floss silk experiment in two colours, 1984
5 x 15 cm

Fig 5.27 Main photo:
Pinebark 2–5 *strip scarves, 2009*
Silk collections, linens, textured yarns
132 x 9–13 cm

unobtrusively controlled by 'knocking it on the head' with whole-stitch, pin, whole-stitch, which will send it back in the opposite direction.

As an example, the pairs prepared for *Snow Leopard*, page 84, where each of the first pins carried one linen and one textured pair, were laid out to shade from light values at the edges to dark in the middle. The shades were then allowed to mingle in the lace but as soon as one looked as if it would stray into the wrong grouping it was directed back.

Many of the pieces in this book have been made by following traditional Torchon rules in order to see what would happen, in the knowledge that this could be altered if necessary. In *Compuswirl I*, page 119, the result was a complete surprise.

However, sometimes one has very definite ideas of the effect one wants. *Compuswirl II* (page 54) was made in a base colour, with lighter threads from the same range added and subtracted where necessary, in order to follow the original inspiration.

My first book (*Pattern Design for Torchon Lace*) advocated the hanging out of one colour in order to add in a second, but it is very much easier to add in a spot colour and work with an extra pair of threads. The ends of the extra colour can be worked into the lace before being cut off, which is also much quicker.

It is possible to design pattern where colour control is part of the system and no extra artifice is needed (as in the *Pinebark* scarves Figs 4.4, 4.8, 5.27 and 7.10), where the pattern dictates that all colours work in vertical stripes. The same happens in *Texture* (Fig 7.17) and *Paintwork* (7.35), where colours remain under close control.

In *Dancing Water* (page 97) they mingle more, and some work right over from one side to another. If made in harmonious colours this is an attractive effect. In *Woodgrain* (page 64), the movement of the colours from inside to outside becomes a whole new system of control.

Principles of Pattern

Fig 6.1 *Below and right:*
Symmetry operations

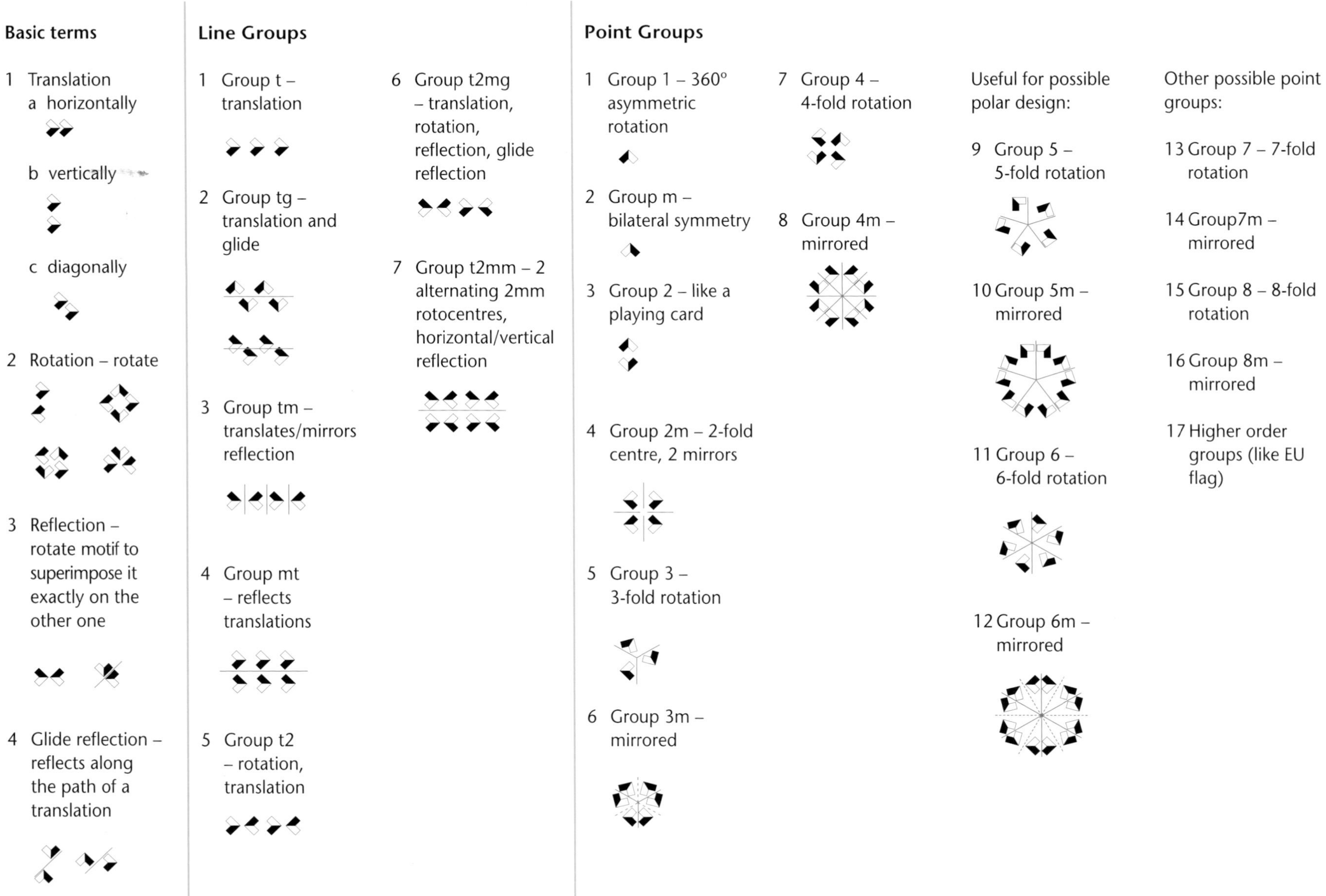

Basic terms

1 Translation
   a horizontally

   b vertically

   c diagonally

2 Rotation – rotate

3 Reflection –
   rotate motif to
   superimpose it
   exactly on the
   other one

4 Glide reflection –
   reflects along
   the path of a
   translation

Line Groups

1 Group t –
   translation

2 Group tg –
   translation and
   glide

3 Group tm –
   translates/mirrors
   reflection

4 Group mt
   – reflects
   translations

5 Group t2
   – rotation,
   translation

6 Group t2mg
   – translation,
   rotation,
   reflection, glide
   reflection

7 Group t2mm – 2
   alternating 2mm
   rotocentres,
   horizontal/vertical
   reflection

Point Groups

1 Group 1 – 360°
   asymmetric
   rotation

2 Group m –
   bilateral symmetry

3 Group 2 – like a
   playing card

4 Group 2m – 2-fold
   centre, 2 mirrors

5 Group 3 –
   3-fold rotation

6 Group 3m –
   mirrored

7 Group 4 –
   4-fold rotation

8 Group 4m –
   mirrored

Useful for possible
polar design:

9 Group 5 –
   5-fold rotation

10 Group 5m –
   mirrored

11 Group 6 –
   6-fold rotation

12 Group 6m –
   mirrored

Other possible point
groups:

13 Group 7 – 7-fold
   rotation

14 Group7m –
   mirrored

15 Group 8 – 8-fold
   rotation

16 Group 8m –
   mirrored

17 Higher order
   groups (like EU
   flag)

Plane Groups

1 Group p1 –
   non-parallel
   translations

2 Group pg –
   2 parallel glide
   reflections

3 Group pm –
   2 parallel mirrors

4 Group cm –
   reflection and
   parallel glide
   reflection

5 Group p2 – 2
   rotations

6 Group p2mg
   – mirror and
   perpendicular
   glide

7 Group p2gg – 2
   perpendicular
   glide reflections

8 Group p2mm
   – rectangle
   bounded by
   mirror lines

9 Group c2mm –
   perpendicular
   mirrors &
   perpendicular
   glide reflections

10 Group p3 –
   3 rotations
   through 120°

11 Group p3m1 –
   reflection of an
   equilateral triangle

12 Group p31m –
   reflection of 120°

13 Group p4 –
   quarter turns

14 Group p4gm
   – reflection of
   quarter turns

15 Group p4mm
   – reflection in
   the sides of a
   45°/45°/90° triangle

16 Group p6 – 6-fold
   rotations

17 Group p6mm
   – reflections
   in the sides of
   a 30°/60°/90°
   triangle

Symmetry

Pattern is used all over the world as a form of communication. It may have religious significance, be traditional symbolism or just be an opportunity to introduce variety into decoration. Both man-made and natural patterns offer huge scope for study, translation and exploitation, although truly original pattern of our own devising should always be the eventual goal.

At its heart is symmetry, derived from the Greek word *symmetria* meaning 'the same measure'. You can twist and turn a symmetrical figure, such as those in Fig 6.1, yet it always remains the same.

Mathematician Marcus du Sautoy has observed: 'The human mind is constantly drawn to anything that embodies some aspect of symmetry. Our brain seems programmed to notice and search for order and structure … Symmetry is about connections between different parts of the same object. It sets up a natural internal dialogue in the shape.'[9]

Symmetry 'operations' underlie pattern design. These are:

- *translation*: vertical and horizontal movement, and diagonal movement also known as 'glide'
- *rotation* around a point
- *reflection* or mirror symmetry
- *glide reflection*.

They provide the basic principles for line, point and plane formations, and are very useful for lace design. All those with relevance to Torchon patterns are detailed on the opposite page (Fig 6.1).

Symmetry operates in far more than visual pattern – it is a meeting point for design, maths, science, psychology and music. (As an example of the last, Bach inverted parts of his *Goldberg Variations* – the notes in the inverted parts are played as if they had been written upside down.)

It extends into 3D with stacking, packing and crystalline structures, and it also forms the basis of natural pattern.

Symmetry can help us in initial design play and as ideas evolve into formal Torchon lace patterns. In addition to the basic operations we can use:

- overlapping
- staggering, stepping
- stripes and pillars
- composite designs (composed of groups of elements)
- interlocking
- regularity and irregularity
- changes of scale or gradation
- texture
- counter-change (the alternation of black and white, as in 'yin and yang')
- drop, brick and wood-block repeats
- lattices and networks built on the square and diamond.

Plane symmetry

Patterns that spread as plane symmetry over a surface, rather than along a linear edging, may be designed for Torchon if we are prepared to expand our work beyond the traditional scale, allowing us to design scarves, screens, curtains and banners.

Wide patterns may be sliced into narrow ones with different uses, including strip scarves and vertical blinds. For example, using the pattern shown on page 106, a lace group could create striking vertical blinds for a community hall, using conventional equipment for strips of lace designed to hang side by side.

If the exercises given from page 89 onwards are combined with thoughtful use of symmetry principles and processes, the lacemaker need never be at a loss for new designs of a completely personal nature.

A natural playing field

When the forces of nature work on an inert substance that is in equilibrium or balance, patterns form spontaneously. For instance, water is the same in all directions until it freezes; then this symmetry is 'broken' into angular and irregular crystals with a special bias to hexagonality. 'Pattern appears when competing forces banish uniformity but cannot quite induce chaos,' Philip Ball has written in *Branches*, one of a series of books on pattern formation in nature.[10]

Glorious patterns organise themselves in the substances that form our natural world: ice, mud, water, bark, stone, wood, vegetation, and on the skins of animals and fish. Each has its own ordering principles whether of growth, drainage, weather, chemical composition or other complex interactions.

The sources are infinite and constantly present themselves as we go about our lives: in the garden, in the forest, on holiday, on the beach, on a walk.

These make fertile fields of exploration for the lace designer. The subtle regularities in these irregular structures allow the isolation of a small section and its repetition over a larger area. The new pattern will have the basic characteristics of the original but as a set of repeated elements it is easier to design and make, and versatile in use.

Once we start to appreciate the possibilities these patterns offer for lace, we can create a diversity of motifs and textures. These may emphasise characteristics that are horizontal, vertical or diagonal, dense or spaced, and allow threads to work through the lace to create different effects.

Some patterns might be particularly suitable for texture, allowing individual threads to display contrasting characteristics (page 93). Some might

beg for smooth continuation around openwork interstices (page 56). Some might encourage threads to spread and mingle (page 97). Some might keep them in tight groups and orders (page 122).

It is possible to subvert designs by making 'game' rules in order to create harmonious informality. The leopard-spot scarf here (Fig 6.2) was created by allowing each spot to be made in the first textured thread to arrive there, but since each spot has a hole in it and needs a second worker, an extra pair was wound in the same texture. The planning is therefore dependent on the passage of threads, although it can be altered at whim if regularity threatens or a certain texture gets left out. The design was first explored with printing (Fig 6.4a) in imitation of a photographed pelt (Fig 6.3), then gridded and enlarged.

The vertical or horizontal nature of some patterns may be emphasised by making those parts in whole-stitch and clouding other parts with half-stitch (pages 12–13). Alternatively, a mixture of threads can be allowed to dictate stitch texture at random as particular threads reach pattern areas (page 109).

Each pattern's characteristics need to be distinctive in order to be individual. Designs can otherwise end up looking fairly similar.

However, some natural patterns may be explored without drawing up a formal design. *Slice of Ice*, page 112, was developed from crystal formations in an ice sheet stranded on a river bank. Shapes from photographs were copied as scribbles and lace worked over these as seemed suitable to test the process. The final piece was constructed in a variety of sparkling filaments to create icy textures.

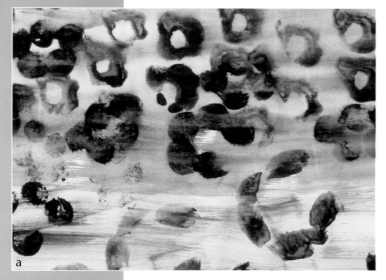

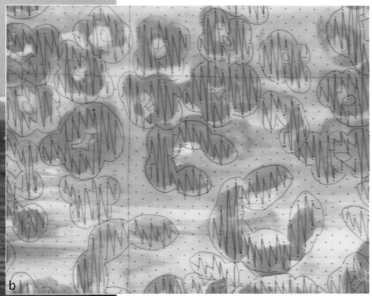

***Fig 6.2** Main photo, left:*
Snow Leopard 1, *2007*
Black and white linen tow 4, 16/2
and others, with 50% textural knitting yarns
166 x 49 cm
Snow Leopard 2, *2008*
Private collection

***Fig 6.3** Inset:*
Leopard pelt

Fig 6.4 a and b
Above:
Leopard print: foam rubber, poster paint and teabags and a pattern tracing

Principles of order

Although the study of the 'self-similarity' and the ordering principles behind natural pattern is a fairly new one, fascination with the hidden rules in nature has always been there and it was Aristotle who suggested that some things do not alter in shape, except by becoming larger, as they grow.

The understanding of pattern formation in nature has developed markedly over the past twenty years, since the advent of computers allowed conjecture to be modelled and resolved. This can give us pointers for the development of lace patterns, and our delicate structures are an excellent medium in which to explore and display natural phenomena.

Aristotle was one of the first to make detailed nature studies and used the word 'gnomons' to describe growth shapes where new tissue is added to old (Fig 6.6). This can be seen in the Nautilus shell section on page 38, and in other shells and horns.

If we can understand some of the underlying principles in operation, we can use them to work out why some designs work better than others and identify useful characteristics to include in new ones.

As an example, there are similar growth processes at work in the *Meteor* pattern (Fig 6.5) to those in *Nautilus*. Pattern elements *dilate* but stay the same shape, as with the gnomon. Patterns that repeat or subtly change similar shapes can have a satisfying sense of unity about them, which may be the reason why this has been the most commercially successful pattern I have sold.

In addition, in *Meteor* the principles at work combine *dilation* with *rotation* – each motif climbs from the centre by stepping back down the grid to allow a slow spiral to develop. Other pattern elements and fancy stitches have been added but only within this ordered system.

Spirals may be 'Archimedean', with parallel lines, or logarithmic, dilating as they move from the centre (Fig 6.7). Polar grids offer many opportunities to play with geometric, man-made and natural spiral formations and lace allows these to be lifted off into helix shapes. We can simply keep working round and round by removing the previous work from the pattern, as with the 'doodle' illustrated here (Figs 6.8, 6.9).

The spiral growth of leaves around a plant stem is known as *phyllotaxis*. Seedheads such as the sunflower are also arranged in spirals, and both of these have been found to follow a mathematical progression known as the *Fibonacci Series*. This sets up a pattern in which one number follows from the addition of the previous two, as in: 1, 1, 2, 3, 5, 8, 13 … and so on. We can pursue progressions like this in our designs.

The ultimate in self-similarity are fractals, an area where maths has captured popular imagination. Fractals show that natural formations can build from minute shapes in which each is a replica of the whole thing. The fern leaf is a good example, for each lobe is a tiny example of the whole frond.

Self-organisation occurs not just in inert systems such as ice crystals but also in biological systems. Examples include animal pelts and the growth of lichen and fungi. It influences the way bees build their colonies, ants build their nests and birds fly in flocks. Research is showing that fish swimming in closely organised schools use continuously monitored positive feedback to move in synchrony. Natural rules govern how close and how far apart individuals like to be, and even why fireflies flash in synchrony.

Once patterns like these capture the imagination, design inspiration will quickly follow. It is the artist within us all who can use them to open the eyes of others to obscured glories by interpreting and revealing them in an individual way.

Fig 6.5 Right:
Meteor, 1993
Linen 60/2
27 cm diameter
First pub: Lace Express

Below, from l to r:
Fig 6.6
Gnomon growth

Fig 6.7
Spirals: Archimedean and logarithmic

Fig 6.8
*Doodle pattern.
The lace was made between different pairs of lines on each circuit*

Fig 6.9 *Inset:*
*Helical doodle, 2003
Silk and steel
116 x 5 cm
Private collection*

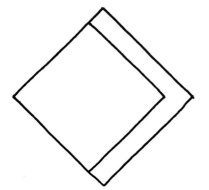
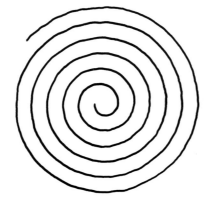
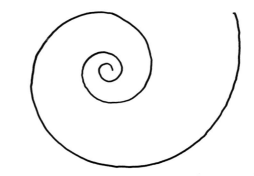
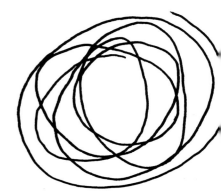

7

Playing with Design

Geometric pattern making

Children play naturally, without thought of any outcome. This is the way to explore geometric pattern. Adults will be tempted to add a little method, but the best way is to relax and see what happens.

The symmetry groupings in the previous chapter show that there are many formations that can be used in the search for new patterns, but these are only part of the story.

Nothing beats quiet exploration with some form of printing. Keep trying, be prolific and see what emerges. Edit out patterns that do not prove inspiring and concentrate on the best ones. It may take a number of tries, but eventually a pattern with good potential will emerge.

Printing can be quick and simple once we have cut a block. We might use a cut potato and poster paint, rubber stamps and a stamp pad, lino and ink, neoprene stuck to a piece of polystyrene, or foam rubber (the kind used for yoga mats has a

good consistency) on an MDF block. We also need plenty of cheap paper and a knife or scissors to cut our stamp.

If the designs are explored in a style and orientation that suits Torchon lace, easily translatable Torchon patterns can be created right from the start. This means working on the diagonal, with groups of block-shapes that would fit onto Torchon grid. Do not forget to overlap and stagger the prints, twist and turn the block using the symmetry operations (see pages 82–83), and try many alternatives in order to create a wide variety of possibilities.

A good starting point is to draw a diamond, one side of which is the length of two or three large squares of graph paper (25–50 mm depending on your grid) with some simple shapes inside (Fig 7.1). The examples on this page have been drawn over 2:10:20 mm grid with at least 2 mm between each shape. You can also draw ideas on a dotted grid, but remember to leave space between one

pattern block and the next.

Shapes do not have to form a recognisable 'pattern' motif, just a juxtaposition of blocks which have potential for development. Good pattern formations can emerge from quite simple groupings (Figs 7.2, 7.3). The more you play in this way, the more you learn about using the process to generate original designs (Fig 7.4).

Note: The sponge rubber and plastic handles used in the illustrations are available from www.contemporarylace.com

Fig 7.1 Below left: Stamp shapes to cut from graph paper

Figs 7.2 and 7.3
Below and right: Pattern development

Fig 7.4 *Main photo: Torchon squares, 1994 and 2009*
White Bockens linen 40/2 and pink Bockens weaving linen 16/1, but the same 1/10 in. grid
White 25 cm²; pink 27 cm²
Patterns developed from the illustrated shapes
First pub: Lace Express (white mat)

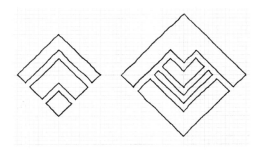

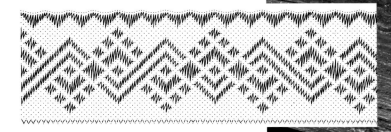

Fig 7.5 Left:
*Straight pattern with
corner*

Fig 7.6 Right:
'Turnover' to match

Fig 7.7 Inset far right:
*Pattern translated to
polar grid (very slight
alteration needed to fit
to required repeat)*

Fig 7.8 Main photo:
*Tablemat, 2006
Bockens linen 16/2
44 x 21 cm
First pub: Lace Express*

Fig 7.9 Below:
*Sectional design would
allow extra repeats to
be inserted to extend
the project into a
runner*

Drafting practice

Drafting patterns is a simple business,
either by joining up dots or drawing from
corner to corner over graph paper. When
working on graph paper, remember to
jump two intersections when moving
horizontally or vertically. Take special
care with this when drawing motifs at a
distance from each other because it is all
too easy to end up with pattern elements
that do not synchronise.

Corners can be created by running a
handbag mirror or mirror tile diagonally
along a straight edging until pattern
shapes form a pleasing right-angled
configuration (Fig 7.5). Patterns with
movement in them, which proceeds
in one direction or another, can be
reversed at the corner, but that means
that a 'turnover' motif will be needed
somewhere along the next length in
order to reverse the pattern into the next
corner (Fig 7.6). This does not need to
be in the centre; the pattern could even
change direction directly after the corner.

Edgings and footsides may be gathered
from existing patterns, or new ones
created. Design just one fan edging and
copy it along the length of a pattern –
it will soon become second nature to
draw the swoops and dips that you find
attractive. To work out whether a fan
needs extending over three, four, five
or more dots, count the number of dots
along a pattern repeat and adjust up or
down, or change to a combination of
large and small fans, to make it fit.

Some patterns will extend to infinity
if space allows, and a decision has to be
made as to how long they should be.
However, a pattern can also be designed
so that it becomes sectional and able to
be extended or shortened (Figs 7.8, 7.9).
Preferably, several different variations
should be tried using coloured pens and
tracing paper to find the best solution
before committing to thread.

Patterns may be drafted at a scale that
fits our favourite threads, or enlarged and
reduced on the photocopier. Since copiers
may distort a pattern slightly, corners
should always be drafted whole.

By drafting our own patterns, we
are able to design lace that exactly fits
our lifestyle, instead of being confined
by traditional or published patterns.
Geometric design is examined in greater
detail in *Pattern Design for Torchon Lace*[1].

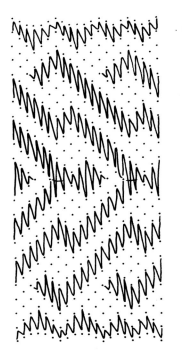

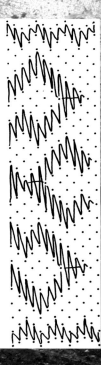

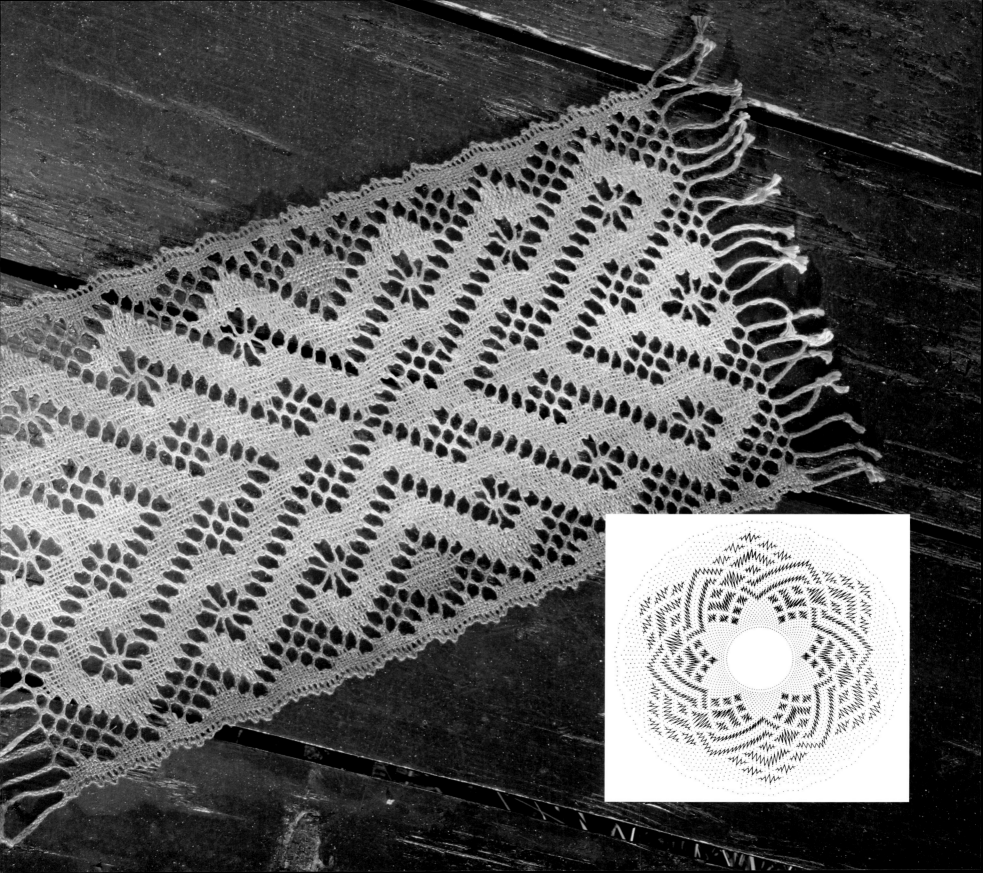

Abstraction

We have seen that a small section of a natural pattern, especially one with a strong and interesting character, can be extended over a surprisingly wide surface area.

The process is simple if taken step by step.

1 First, find (or create) a pattern.
2 Record it and simplify it.
3 Translate it to a grid that allows the right amount of detail to be included.
4 Draft a square, rectangular or diamond-shaped area.
5 Tessellate it (like wallpaper) and smooth out the joins.
6 Prove that the pattern works.

Let us look first at how the pattern for the scarf opposite (Fig 7.10) was created, to gain an overview, and then look at alternative methods on the following pages.

Pinebark came from a rubbing from the bark of a pine tree (Fig 7.11). The distinctive shapes suggested a pattern of vertical trails, but a different pattern could also be drafted on the diagonal.

Bark rubbings usually being indistinct, it is good to trace round the shapes and shade them in (Fig 7.12), so that the characteristics of the pattern may easily be seen. This one was too small for the 1 cm grid I usually use for this type of design, so it was enlarged on the photocopier at several different sizes. Evaluation could then be made of the version that would best bring out the character of the source material (Fig 7.13). This size of pattern may easily be enlarged or reduced to suit a wide range of threads.

The chosen size allowed narrow whole-stitch trails to be drafted over the bark shapes. Once a full A3 page of pattern had been drafted, it was divided up into vertical rectangular sections a, b, c and d which could be tessellated into a 'wallpaper' pattern (Fig 7.14). (See 'Tessellation' page 98 for the full explanation of this.)

Where these sections are joined to a new area of pattern, the motifs can usually be 'tidied up' to create a balanced design which flows seamlessly from one section to the next. In this case, small fussy trails were also amalgamated (Fig 7.15) and empty areas filled.

The indigo scarf used only the centre section, but the pattern could be joined for large items such as a curtain. Narrow sections have proved useful for strip-scarves in a wide variety of colourways and yarns, enlarged or reduced to suit the chosen materials (see Figs 4.4, 4.9 and 5.27 and yarn tables on pages 134–37 for guidance).

Fig 7.10 Main photo: Pinebark scarf, 2009 Indigo-dyed linen, cotton, rayon and silk 150 x 25 cm

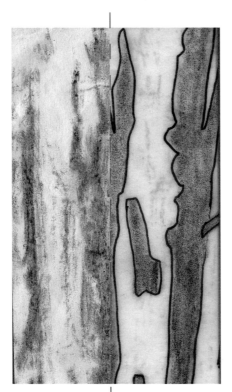

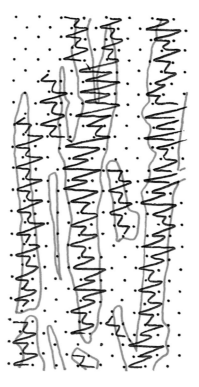

This page from l to r:
***Fig 7.11** Bark rubbing*

***Fig 7.12** Rubbing, traced and shaded on the right-hand side*

***Fig 7.13** Pattern fitted to grid*

***Fig 7.14** Tessellation chosen*

Opposite:
Fig 7.15 a and b
Top: Over-complicated details simplified

***Fig 7.16** Pinebark pattern*

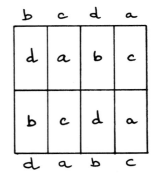

a

b

93

Fig 7.17 Main photo: Texture *scarf, 1996 Aran-weight linen, cotton and wool 150 x 29 cm*

Insets opposite:
Fig 7.18 Top: *Photo of the trunk of a tree*

Fig 7.19 Below: *Exploration on acetate*

This page:
Fig 7.20 Top left: *The acetate on its own*

Fig 7.21 Centre left: *Mark making with charcoal*

Fig 7.22 Bottom left: *Stencil cut from charcoal marks*

Fig 7.23 Bottom right: *Photo with intriguing sunlight reflections*

Fig 7.24 Far right: *Similar shapes created by cutting and rubbing card*

Recording and simplification

Once identified, a natural pattern will need to be captured. This can be done by using photography, wax rubbings, tracings with paper, film or acetate, drawing, painting and pastel painting, or we can create our own patterns with mark making.

Patterns often seem too cluttered with detail. Depending on the size of the pattern, and the equipment available, there are various ways to deal with this:

- As has been shown, a wax rubbing may be simplified by tracing and shading.
- A photograph (Fig 7.18) could be explored through acetate using a permanent pen to trace off shapes (Fig 7.19). This was another way of exploiting bark patterns, used as the basis for the *Sycamore* pattern.
- A patch of mark making (Fig 7.21) might be explored with a stencil (Fig 7.22) cut around individual marks and then enlarged as pattern motifs. This was the start of the *Texture* pattern.

- More elusive patterns may require their major features to be worked up in a new way. The card rubbing in Fig 7.24 was a way of recreating on paper the haphazard configuration of sunlight reflections captured in a photograph (Fig 7.23), which became the pattern for the *Dancing Water* design.

In each case, the objective is to tease out the basic shapes so that they may easily be married with a grid. A small sheet of card was slashed diagonally, reassembled and then rubbed under thin paper several times. This caused the pieces to displace in a more informal pattern.

A tracing may be placed over a printed grid, or a traced grid may be placed over a drawing or photocopy. Depending on the pattern required, positive or negative shapes may be used – in *Sycamore* the pattern was drawn into the spaces around the traced shapes, but for *Texture* it was the shapes themselves which became the pattern motifs.

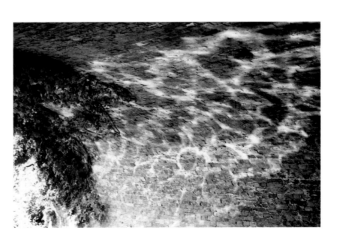

Translation to grid

To fit a pattern to a grid we need a little practice or experience to help our judgement and the way to learn is to put the process into action.

Essentially, the key is to find a grid which will allow the maximum amount of information that delivers the character of our source material:

- If the grid is too small, the pattern will end up needlessly complicated.
- If it is too big, it may lose the character of the design.
- If it is just right, a pattern can be designed that is easy to develop and make.

Work at the scale that suits you best. The smaller the grid, the longer the lace will take to make but it will be more suitable for traditional equipment. I prefer to use a 1 cm grid on A3 for large-scale work, as this is easy to enlarge for scarves, but such patterns can also be very pretty in finer threads on smaller grids. A 5 mm grid on A4 paper will capture more detail in smaller pattern motifs, and this can be enlarged or redrafted onto larger grid. In all cases, the original inspiration and the grid size need to be carefully matched.

Shown here is an example of how the source material from the previous page was fitted to grid using this method. The bark acetate used as the basis for the *Sycamore* pattern was enlarged on the photocopier at a greatly increased size.

Since it was the smooth flow of the bark around the clefts that inspired the pattern, the spaces in between the motifs were drafted with trails, and the gaps were left as ground, later modified as honeycomb where suitable (Fig 7.27, lace Fig 4.5).

In the *Texture* pattern derived from mark making (lace Figs 7.17 and 7.36), the marks explored with stencilling

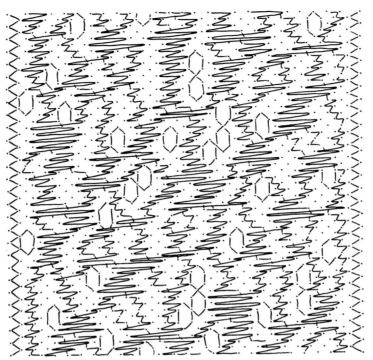

remained too small for the pattern process so similar shapes were drawn freehand at a size suitable for resolution with the large grid. The *Dancing Water* pattern transferred easily to grid (Fig 7.25).

Drafting

Once the source material fits its grid, we can draft a page of pattern. First draw Torchon trails to cover the areas identified as whole- or half-stitch, and leave the rest as grid. It may help to draw horizontal lines first and join them up with the diagonals afterwards. When choosing dots, go to the one closest to the motif, but keep the option of making different decisions if the pattern loses its character.

A3 tracing paper and a 1 cm grid give plenty of room for a pattern to unroll; A4 would need a smaller grid and more detailed pattern. When the page is complete, we are ready for tessellation.

Fig 7.25 Main photo: Dancing Water *scarf, 1998
Linen tow 4 and various cotton and silk knitting yarns with metallic
190 x 32 cm (excl. fringes)
First pub:* Lace Express

Fig 7.26 Right: *Pattern drafted around bark shapes,* Sycamore *pattern*

Fig 7.27 Left: Sycamore *pattern modified with honeycomb*

Fig 7.28 Below left: *Redrawn texture marks with their Torchon trails*

Fig 7.29 Below: Dancing Water *card shapes with trails mapped around them*

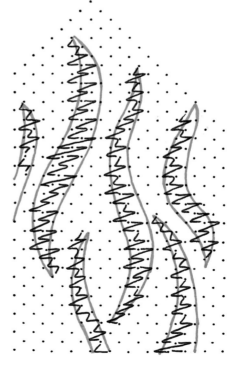
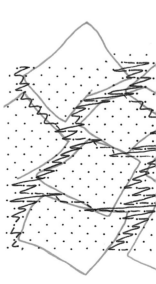

Tessellation

Tessellation involves spreading a pattern in all directions. Pattern will tessellate easily on a Torchon grid if divided into repeatable blocks that are:

- square (Fig 7.30)
- rectangular, whether horizontal (Fig 7.31) or vertical (Fig 7.14) or
- diamond-shaped (Fig 7.32).

It may be sensible to tessellate the whole, or an especially attractive section, of the page of pattern that has been created.

The basic process involves drawing a shape that can be divided into four sections, numbering these, and then repeating each piece on the opposite side of the shape by copying each section. It might seem easier to photocopy the pattern, cut it up and arrange the pieces, but sadly this can be more trouble than it is worth because errors can so easily happen and the dots may not match up.

With a little time and care, the pattern can be fitted to the Torchon grid by moving the pattern by hand and eye. This might seem laborious and the dots will have to be counted carefully, but this is the only part of the process that needs such patience.

Proving the pattern

Once a square, rectangular or diamond-shaped tessellation has been completed, there will be areas where the pattern breaks up at the joins (Fig 7.33); the task now is to smooth those areas over by altering the drafting so that the pattern carries on evenly (Fig 7.34). Just choose what seems to be the best solution; notice that the same problem occurs twice in each pattern, so (to save time) the solution can be copied from one place to another (Fig 7.32). In Fig 7.35 you can still see the 'ghost' of the original diamond.

When that is complete, the resultant pattern will repeat lengthways and sideways, allowing it to be made any size desired. If tessellated sideways, the pattern will have to be joined over the vertical break, but there will already be a template to follow inside the pattern (Fig 7.32).

Pinebark was tessellated with vertical rectangles, *Dancing Water* with horizontal rectangles (only the central part of the pattern being illustrated, Fig 7.25), and the *Texture* and *Sycamore* patterns used diamond-shaped tessellation.

Part of the choice involved the size of the finished pattern and ease of photocopying if enlargement was required. Pattern drafted to fit on A4 (or drafted to split in A4-sized halves) will be cheaper to enlarge to A3/141%, a useful size for scarves, than if drafted A3 and enlarged to A2.

A tessellated pattern could become the curtain for a door, if you have enough bobbins and a pillow to fit it, or a narrow belt or hat band. Extra edges or selvedges may be added as required.

Below, from l to r:
Fig 7.30
Square tessellation

Fig 7.31
Horizontal rectangular tessellation

Fig 7.32
Diamond-shaped tessellation, with reminder-marks of where the pattern repeats

Fig 7.33 Right: Tessellation in progress, with gaps to fill

Fig 7.34 Below right: Shapes enlarged to fill space

Fig 7.35 Inset opposite: Texture pattern

Fig 7.36 Main photo: Texture cushion, 1997 Weaving linen and textured knitting cottons 42 x 40 cm

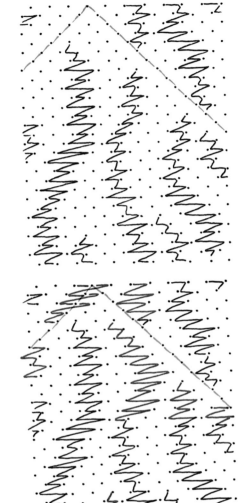

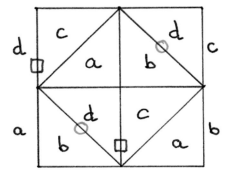

c	d	c	d
b	a	b	a
c	d	c	d
b	a	b	a

a	b
d	c
a	b
d	c

8 Practical Stylisation

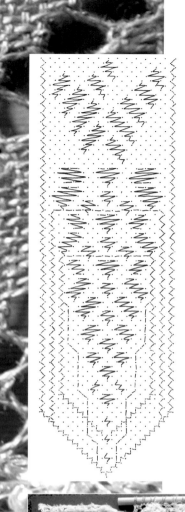

Wisteria

Flowers and leaves have always been part of lace design, although not of Torchon. To make them suitable for the square grid this lace uses, we have to simplify them into *stylised* geometric shapes.

The process of stylisation aims to convey the spirit of the subject and to keep it just about recognisable, while fitting it to the limits of the medium in which we are working. Flowing lines have to be straightened, and curves become corners.

We can see this process in the decorative details that Arts and Crafts designers like Charles Rennie Mackintosh and Frank Lloyd Wright added to their architecture, as did A W N Pugin, whose ornamental Gothic designs are found throughout the House of Commons. All three took their ideas from nature.

Wright's 'light screens' at the Susan Lawrence Dana House, Springfield, Illinois, include sumac blossom rendered as chevrons of iridescent glass (Fig 8.1). They were the inspiration for my own studies in stylisation for lace which started with a plant often admired in other decorative arts, the wisteria.

After examining a number of different plants, my approach to the wisteria was to:

- study a plant closely by drawing it
- simplify from the start by cutting out any unnecessary detail, choosing the lines and shapes that best portrayed the subject
- draw the shapes in an angular manner that would transfer more easily to the grid (Fig 8.2)
- turn the petals and leaves into geometric shapes
- keep a careful record of the colours involved, using photography (or painting) (Fig 8.3).

Wisteria has large racemes (hanging groups of flowers). Since arranging and overlapping these in a design for a panel would be complicated, the alternative was to make the racemes separately, as individual hangings, and arrange them as an informal group on a trellis (Fig 8.6).

Although a wisteria in bloom displays flowers at different stages in their development, just one pattern could be interpreted in a number of different sizes and styles (Fig 8.4), some as small blooms, some as large ones with leaves. Each raceme can look different from the next yet is only a variation on a theme.

To shade the flowers, a variety of knitting, weaving and embroidery yarns were carefully sorted to achieve subtle gradation and arranged on a sample card to aid placement in the work (Fig 8.5). Each piece was set up in green linen and the flowers were added by hanging in pairs of bobbins with short lengths of yarn. Leaves were worked in the base thread, as required.

This pattern could be adapted for similar kinds of flowers, such as a laburnum in shades of yellow, or made with pink or white for different kinds of wisteria. The panels could be arranged horizontally over an arch or vertically down a wall.

Fig 8.1 Below: Frank Lloyd Wright, 1903
Rendered by Dennis Casey, 1997
Art glass from hanging sumac blossom, Susan Lawrence Dana House, Springfield, Illinois

Fig 8.2 Far left: Wisteria blossoms, half-stylised as they were drawn

Fig 8.3 Far left, below: Photo used as colour study

Fig 8.4 This page, top left: Wisteria pattern allowing many different interpretations

Fig 8.5 Bottom left: Threads arranged in shade graduation

Fig 8.6 Main photo: Wisteria, 2003
Linen 16/2 with mixed embroidery and knitting yarns
Panels max. 47 x 14 cm, min. 24 x 10 cm

Roses

Some stylised shapes have been used so often that they have become symbols – we know that the spiral in the knitting pattern in Fig 8.7 is a rose, because we are so familiar with it.

We can find many other examples, such as that on the John Galliano dress in Fig 8.8. The spiral rose became a particularly personal motif for Charles Rennie Mackintosh whose Glasgow roses show a variety of spiral arrangements of the basic arced petals (Fig 8.9).

Exploring ready-stylised shapes can be tackled without drawing from life:

- Draw freehand.
- Explore variations to find an attractive shape (Fig 8.10).
- Try out on various grid configurations.
- Redraft each time – it will not transfer dot-to-dot from square to polar grid, for example.
- A good shape may be cut down for smaller spaces (Fig 8.11).
- The design may be shaded with different stitches, such as half-stitch and whole-stitch (Fig 8.12).
- In the *Spiral Rose* mat, shade variations were also alternated to add variety.

Whereas the spiral depicts a rose in full bloom, the *Rose Tray* (Fig 8.13) was designed from a photograph of a developing bud. The flower is tighter and more angular and was designed, like the wisteria, by drawing shapes into the grid, rather than fitting a grid to the shape, as with the spiral.

The many types of roses, from the simple wild rose to the full-blown hybrid, have led to many styles of design. One of the most familiar will be the Tudor rose, historically created by fitting one wild white rose inside a red one to create a symbol of national unity.

This design therefore has strong links to monarchy, and the golden rose displayed here (Fig 8.12) was created at the time of the Golden Jubilee of Queen Elizabeth II, inspired by a knitting pattern published for her Coronation.

The rose can be shaded by hanging in pale threads at the centre and darker ones towards the outside. This method also allows the pattern to be made up in the two traditional colours of red and white, although this would be a much starker contrast.

Fig 8.7 Top right: Spiral motifs in a *Prima* knitting pattern

Fig 8.8 Centre right: Spiral embroidery on a John Galliano dress

Bottom row from l to r:
Fig 8.9 Mackintosh rose

Fig 8.10 Spiral rose motif, which can be modified and reduced on a necklace grid

Fig 8.11 Rose reduced for necklace

Fig 8.12 Main photo:
Spiral Rose, 2001
Golden Jubilee Rose, 2003
Pink linen 60/3 and yellow linen 40/2 with 50/4
27 cm diameter

Fig 8.13 Inset:
Rose Tray, 2001
Linen 50/3
29 x 19 cm
First pub: Lace Express

Virginia creeper

Each autumn, a barn beside a local highway glowed red as its Virginia creeper turned in colour. This was the starting point for a project to create a layered hanging from a fall of foliage.

The subject was recorded with photography and a length of creeper was cut for study in greater depth by drawing.

We can gain confidence in drawing with this simple 'loosening-up' exercise:

■ Draw the plant or flower but look only at the subject, not at the drawing. It does not matter that this is a mess!

■ Now draw it again, looking at both subject and drawing – often successful because we have looked at the subject so closely to begin with.

The whole branch of creeper was drawn, leaf by leaf, to create a library of shapes, sizes and orientations. Reference photos were also taken, and the colours studied before the plant disintegrated (although it lasted several days in damp newspaper).

Design work then developed through various stages:

■ The drawings were traced, photocopied and slightly enlarged.
■ They were used as templates for card cut-outs, which were arranged and assessed as a new fall of creeper.
■ The collage was rubbed with coloured wax on rice paper to gauge the overall effect (Fig 8.14).
■ It was traced as a pattern template then gridded as lace.
■ It was sampled and assessed (Fig 8.15).

The thread being used for the project was Bockens 16/2 weaving linen, in greens, reds, yellows and browns. Samples were made in both single and double thread, but the latter (Fig 8.17) needs very simple design to be successful.

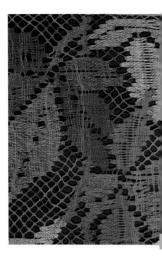

This naturalistic way of creating a lace design proved too dense to layer – partly because the leaf shapes overlapped, and some thread had been doubled to heighten the colours. So it was back to the drawing board. Because the leaves in this project are quite complicated, it was decided to focus on single threads, with honeycomb grid for speed.

■ Stylised leaf designs were eventually tessellated over two, three, four, five and six squares of the grid (Fig 8.16).
■ A sample was assessed (Fig 8.18).
■ They were again too dense, difficult to resolve colourwise, and 'too-clever-by-half'.
■ But the self-similar leaf designs were suitable for spreading out in a hanging.

A large log grid was chosen, one panel to be configured with leaves, the other plain. This gave a moiré effect, the two grids 'interfering' and twinkling as the viewer walked past. Colour placement was inspired by a creeper photographed on a visit abroad (Fig 8.19).

The process was lengthy but it provided a body of work from which many other ideas could be drawn. The project is shown in full on page 27 (Fig 3.9), and in detail in Fig 8.20.

Fig 8.14 Left: Collage rubbed in coloured wax

Fig 8.15 This page, top right: Foliage panel – far too dense

Fig 8.16 Below right: Leaf designs on honeycomb grid

Next page, from top: *Fig 8.17* Doubled thread: bolder lace needs simple motifs

Fig 8.18 Tessellated leaf panel

Fig 8.19 Creeper in Bern, Switzerland

Fig 8.20 Main photo: Under the Red Bough I & II, *detail*

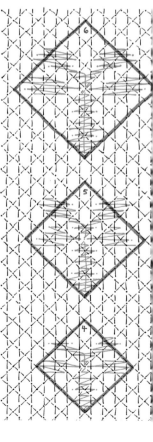

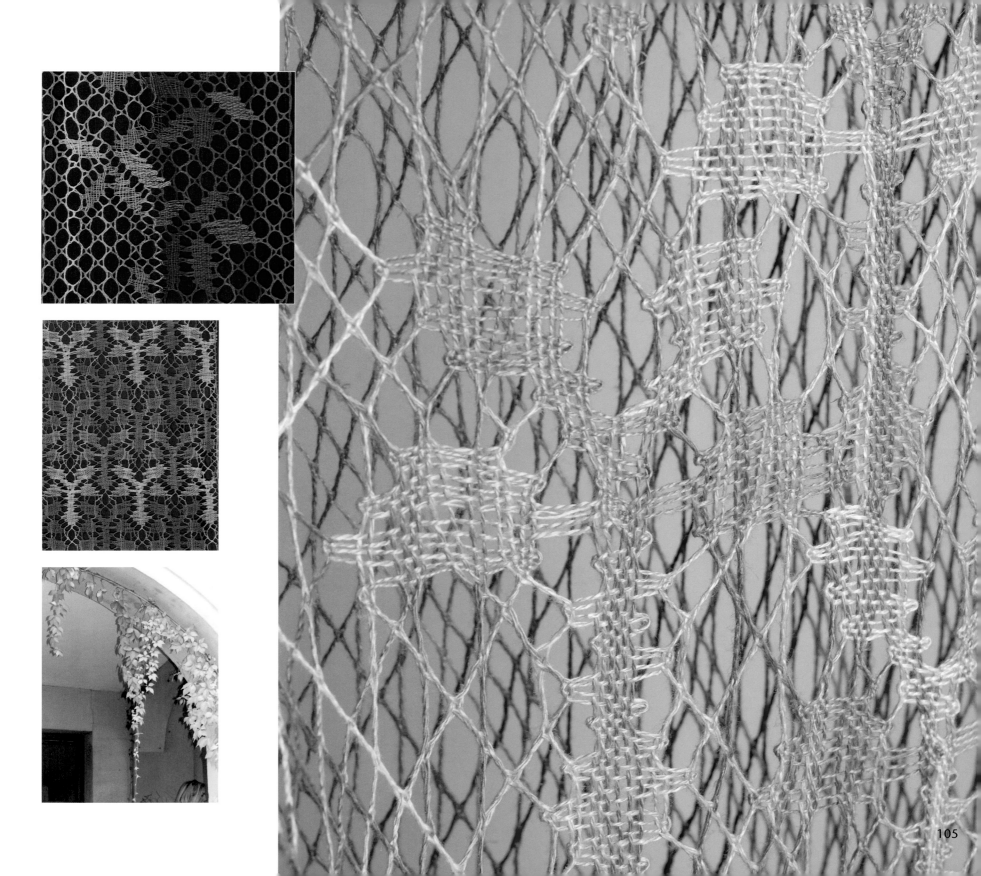

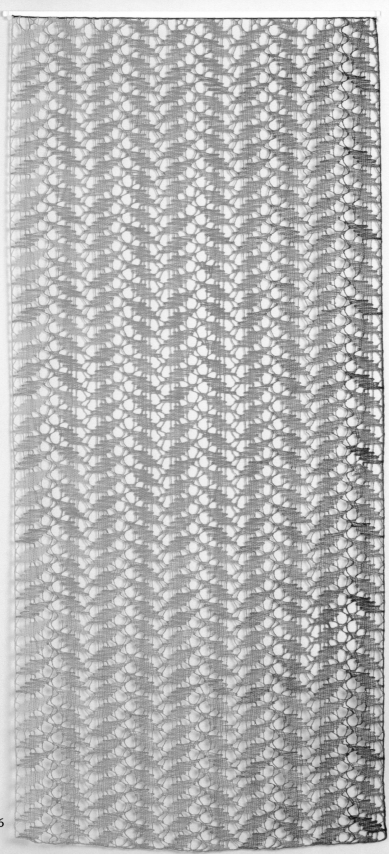

Tree of life

One of the designs that emerged from the body of work around the hanging creeper (page 105, Fig 8.17, which led to Fig 8.21) was an arrangement of shapes which I was beginning to recognise elsewhere. It suggests a very simple leaf, and appears in many cultures in an area that may loosely be described as the 'tree of life'.

I noticed them in books, in graphic design, and even picked up one example – a greetings card – on a tube station floor (Fig 8.22). Now conscious of them, I continue to see new versions – they may appear as complete trees, sometimes just as upward-springing foliage.

- The shapes may be rounded or pointed, as are leaves themselves.
- Designs may have varying degrees of complexity.
- Leaves may alternate as pairs.
- Shapes may have one overall orientation (as used in *Polka*, page 52).

There is only so far one can go when designing lace before it becomes imperative to make it up to see what might happen – a vital part of any experimental process.

It proved intriguing to sample this pattern as the process revealed a cyclical repeat of the worker threads that make the motifs. Four colours repeat in each column.

A panel was made first in contrasting colours, but this did not seem to use the pattern to its full potential (Fig 8.26). However, using the knowledge gained, it was possible to shade a wider piece across its width by changing one colour at a time in each column. If carefully planned so that each thread was hung in at the correct place, the lacemaking would be completely straightforward.

The colours in the Bockens range are quite strong and bright, but I wanted to see if I could make a subtle effect (Fig 8.21). The project was first drawn out in coloured pen to make sure the effect would work (Fig 8.24). This took a couple of hours, which seemed a sensible precaution for a piece that would take 60 hours to make.

The creeper project also diverted along other paths, including the exploration of bare stems in plaits and bars (Fig 8.25). This led to stranded necklaces (Fig 8.27) and paved the way for *Slice of Ice* (page 112).

Work has to continue until it gives back the feeling we are looking for. This may take time to think through, but with lace we often cannot be sure how things will turn out until we make it, and possibly remake it to iron out problems.

Fig 8.21 Far left:
Under the Red Bough
IV, *2005*
Linen 16/2
133 x 56 cm
Winner of Teachers'
Trophy, Lace Guild
Seven exhibition, 2007

Fig 8.22 Left:
Basic tree of life
patterns from Zeitgeist

Next page
Fig 8.23 Top left:
The carefully worked-
out starting point, which
included thread shading

Fig 8.24 Top right:
Pattern planning in
coloured pens

Fig 8.25 Bottom left:
Bare stems explored in
bars and plaits

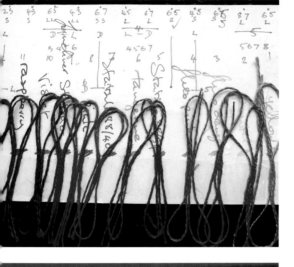

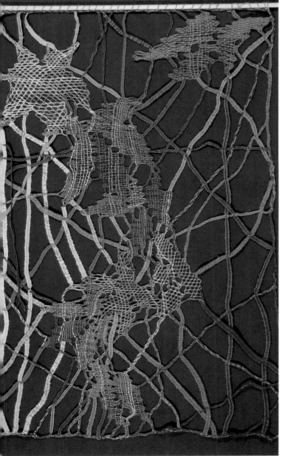

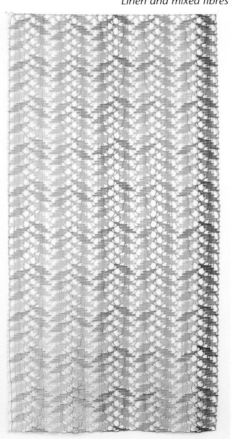

Fig 8.26 Below:
Under the Red Bough
III

Fig 8.27 Right:
Stranded necklace,
2002
Linen and mixed fibres

Birch

Birch had been in mind, but not on paper, for some time before I visited 78 Derngate, Northampton. This was once the home of a local industrialist, and now features the restoration of an interior decoration scheme devised for him in 1916 by Charles Rennie Mackintosh. At no.78, geometric stylisation of birch trees stencilled onto black walls makes a striking statement (Fig 8.28).

Yellow triangles had been used to suggest leaves, with chequered columns for trunks. There were parallels with some of the diaper patterns I had previously drawn up for Torchon, and I began to explore and experiment with the following ideas:

- triangles in homage to Mackintosh (Fig 8.29) – but the results were not at all leaf-like
- stylised birch leaves, allowing a mixture of colours to give a dappled effect (Fig 8.30)
- two diamond patterns to explore trunks (Fig 8.31).

When commissioned to create a hanging for a Sussex farmhouse, these ideas were developed further. The client liked the style and texture of the *Bone Lace* project (page 6) which had been worked informally in mixtures of thicker threads, and he thought a shape similar to the creeper hanging would fit with his space, which had a prominent location but needed quiet and subtle treatment.

Exploration of the birch ideas on a much larger grid than before brought up new possibilities:

- Leaves could be spread in informal groupings, with or without branches or trunks.
- Interpretation could develop the *Bone Lace* ideas of allowing threads to dictate how work proceeded.

- If a mixture of threads was evenly distributed at the start, half-stitch leaves would split up the pairs. The threads which then arrived at the start of each leaf could determine the way it would be made: if all four were different, half-stitch would follow the first leader thread, with double-twists at the end of each row to keep the same thread throughout, but if there were matching threads, thick, medium or thin, the leaf would be whole-stitch (unless I changed my mind!).

The result gave a subtle, dappled effect in keeping with the way wind and sunlight would constantly affect leaves on a tree.

- Each project in this chapter built up extra strategies.
- Without the extra knowledge gained from working the *Bone Lace* project, I would never have thought of this way of interpreting *Betula Pendula* (Fig 8.32).
- This approach will lead to future explorations in colour.

Bottom row, from l to r:

Fig 8.28 Stencil design by Charles Rennie Mackintosh for the home of W J Bassett-Lowke at 78 Derngate, Northampton

Fig 8.29 Birch sample 1, 2005
Linen 16/2

Fig 8.30 Birch sample 2

Fig 8.31 Birch sample 3

Main photos:
Fig 8.32 Betula Pendula, 2008
Texere rug warp and Czech linen
135 x 55 cm
Private collection

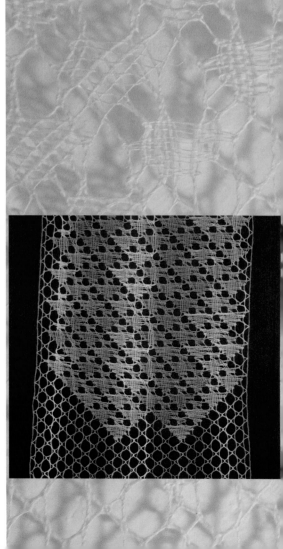

Strategies and Tactics

Design – just child's play

Design is all about problem-solving and, although each situation will be different, strategies can be adapted to provide a variety of solutions. This chapter looks at a number of useful options.

Adults often feel daunted by the very thought of design but, if we can separate the goal from the process, it can be 'child's play'. So the first suggestion is – just relax and *play*.

When we become absorbed by a productive activity we can enter a state that has been called 'flow', when good work becomes effortless because we are in harmony with our task. A good way to move forward is to look back and use those times in childhood when we were encouraged to play with pattern.

Frank Lloyd Wright was one of a generation of designers reared from the nursery on the 'gifts' of Friedrich Froebel, the inventor of 'kindergarten', who was keen that 'every human soul may grow of itself out of its own individuality'. Wright ascribed some of his fluency with pattern (see page 101) to his kindergarten experiences with the 'gifts' (which include building blocks and parquetry shapes) that encourage a child's creativity and spatial awareness. They have long since been absorbed into mainstream infant education.

The mosaic pattern in Fig 9.1 was created during half an hour's undirected parquetry and pattern play in a lace class. There was no goal; students just played with the toys that appealed to them, and explored the pattern motifs on graph paper at a later date. Encouraging results were then produced very quickly.

A completed design appeared at the next class, where one student, Rosemary Atkinson, admitted: 'I couldn't keep my hands off it!' After taking this first piece of lace design through to a finished square of lace, Rosemary then transferred it to a log grid and made that too (Fig 9.2).

Simple kits for pattern play used to be standard stock in toy shops but are not always easy to find in our modern world, although they may surface secondhand. Froebel 'gifts' are still available in wood and cardboard (and can also be home-made), and there are other similar wood and magnetic options (Fig 9.5) as well as computer adaptations; Kaleidodraw by Protozone is an interesting example.

The big advantage with all such toys is that the pieces are easily moved. Designs can be edited and evaluated, destroyed and quickly created anew, with fresh and novel ideas forming all the time. Pieces may be arranged to form geometric borders and diapers, as well as stylised flowers and foliage such as those of the Arts and Crafts and Art Deco designers, and have great potential for transfer to lace (Figs 9.3, 9.4).

Figs 9.1 *Left: Mosaic pattern created during quiet play*

Fig 9.2 *Above: Rosemary Atkinson, 2007 Straight and log grid lace design from mosaic play 23 x 18 cm*

Figs 9.3 and 9.4 *Below, left and right: Parquetry design for polar lace*

Fig 9.5 *Main photo: Froebel 'gift' 7, parquetry Magnetic Mosaics (Nova Design Group) and Circle Fantasy (Spiel & Holz Design)*

A few quiet hours exploring pattern possibilities can be the key that opens the door to design confidence; once through that door, there is no turning back.

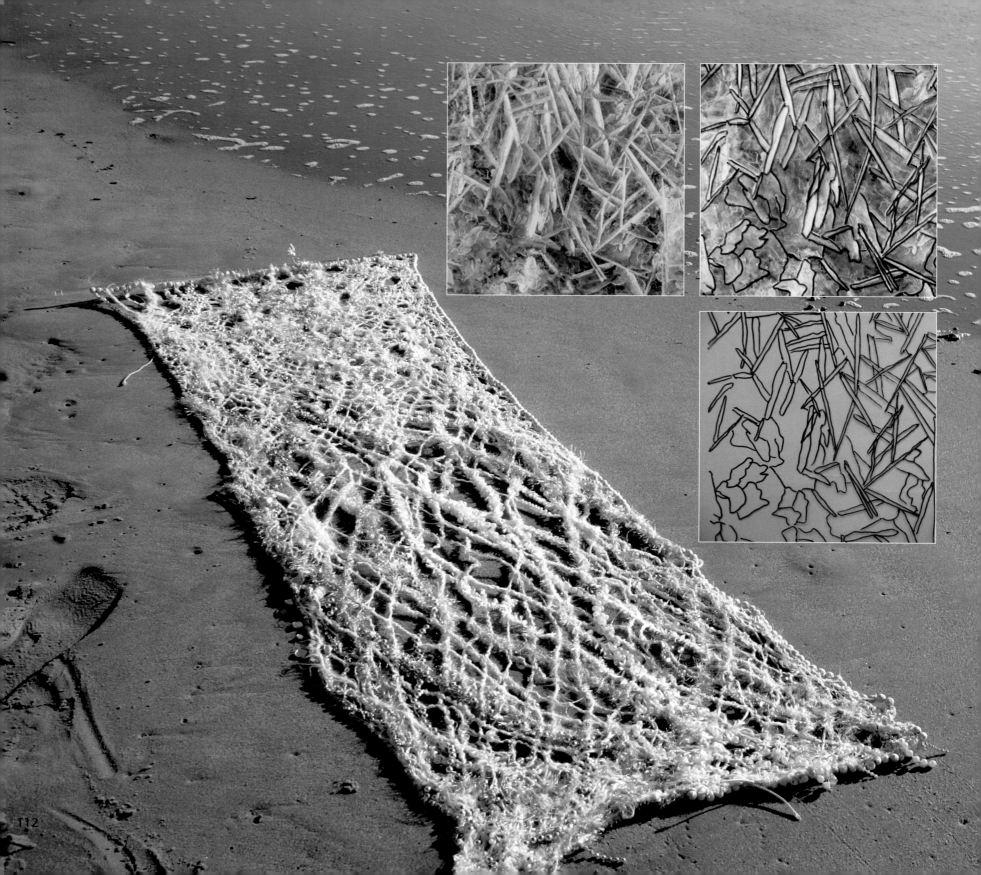

Tactical lacemaking

One problem with gridded designs is that they can stop us acting spontaneously.

Using our wits to solve a new problem can be more stimulating than relying on established rules. Tactics can include inventing new textures based on rhythmical stitch patterns. These will already be familiar, from alternating whole- and half-stitches in 'wild ground', but we can make up our own repeating stitch combinations in the same way that knitters do.

Tiny repetitive patterns might be suitable for a man's tie, or could be used in larger areas to give the effect of fancy weaving. We can make up our own patterns, such as the one created here (Figs 9.10, 9.11).

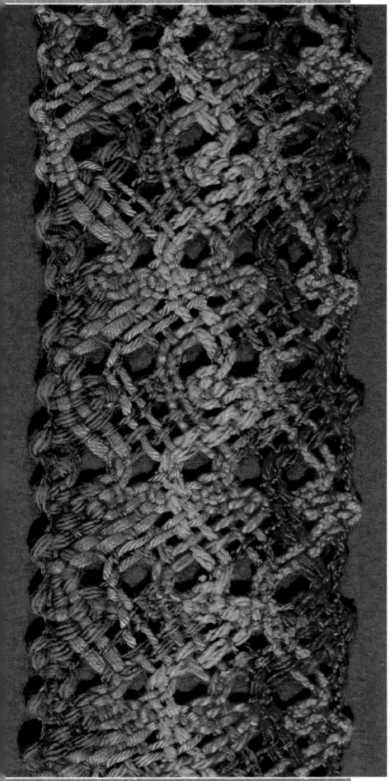

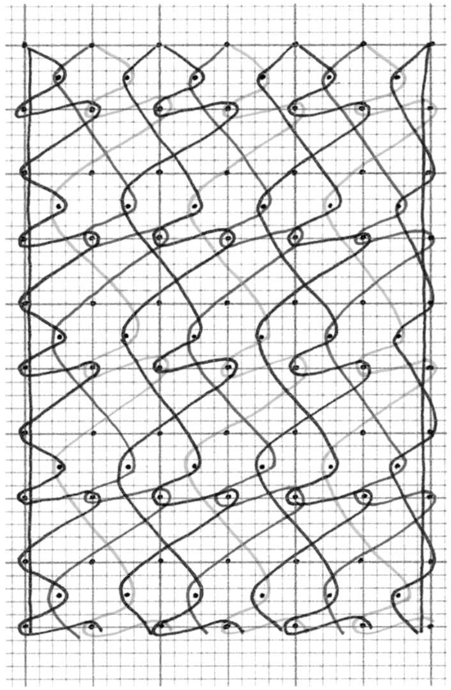

Eight blue pairs were interspersed with three russet and three purple, arranged so that the russet pairs set off to the right and the purple ones to the left, over a 1 cm grid. The instructions have been abbreviated in the manner of a knitting pattern: twist – tw; pair – pr; whole-stitch – wh st.

The following rhythm was then followed:

Setting-in row: at each pin: wh st, tw.
Row 1: tw edge pr; at each pin, wh st, pin, wh st, no tw; tw edge pr.
Row 2: working from the left, work the left-hand pr from the 1st pin in previous row in wh st, pin, wh st, wh st through next pr, wh st next pr, pin, wh st; leave first worker pair, pick up new one from this pin, follow process to end of row.
Row 3: wh st with each 2pr bobbins, no pin.
Row 4: tw edge pr and leave outside pin, wh st each next 2pr but just leave hanging on pins, tw edge pr and leave outside pin.

This kind of pattern works best in plain colours since variegated yarn loses the effect. If made in the shape of a tie pattern, special tie interfacing would complete the project professionally.

Another method of working without a gridded design is to create a spontaneous response to natural patterns and textures on the pillow, by making the lace directly over a photograph or a simplified sketch, diagram or texture exploration. *Slice of Ice* (Fig 9.6) was inspired by a sheet of varied ice crystals stranded on a riverbank, which were then explored on acetate over photo prints. Computer paint programs could be used to develop other possibilities.

Working with the photographs as inspiration, and the photocopied and enlarged acetate as guidelines on the pillow (Figs 9.7, 9.8 and 9.9), the lace was first made as a large sample to test the process. Later it was made as a full piece using several years' accumulation of Christmas filaments, including tinsel and strings of beads, some coiled and tied, some stuck onto bobbins with sticky tape.

By starting *Slice of Ice* in large interconnected sections of half-stitch, all the pairs of threads were split up from the very beginning. Long crystals were interpreted with bars using two pairs, one as passives and the other two woven in and out together. Other pairs were left underneath to retain a basic, diagonal structural web to ensure that threads remained evenly distributed.

This kind of lacemaking requires constant decision making. In normal Torchon, many of the decisions are made as part of a traditional kit of techniques, although quite a high degree of spontaneity can also be incorporated. Planned Torchon can be a comfortable, mechanical and relaxing occupation whereas working spontaneously it is a constant, but enjoyable, challenge.

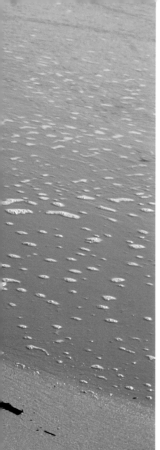

Fig 9.6 *Main photo: Slice of Ice, Christmas Crystals, 2008 Christmas decorations, nylon monofilament, weaving linens and textured knitting yarns 182 x 60 cm*

Figs 9.7, 9.8 and 9.9 *Insets opposite: Ice slice photo with its acetate overlay and photocopy for lacemaking*

Fig 9.10 *This page, far left: Sample for gentleman's tie, 1999 Knitting threads in linen, cotton (russet) and silk (purple)*

Fig 9.11 *Left: Thread diagram*

> **You do not need to draw a pattern to put new ideas into practice; just experiment with promising textures.**

Into the unknown

Stepping beyond our comfort zone can itself be a problem unless something gives us a push. Making familiar lace stitches in an unfamiliar way, as well as exploring new ones, may be one way of doing this.

Making stitches in colour (Fig 9.12) will soon demonstrate how their structure may be exploited. There are now many useful books of stitch collections to be investigated, although Torchon imposes restrictions with its simple square grid. Stitch variations offer shaded effects as well as colour play to add to the complex mix of strategies at your disposal, although care needs to be taken that they do not 'muddy' the effect too much.

Another approach is to accept the technical challenges that natural patterns can reveal. Sometimes useful discoveries can emerge from what appears to be a straightforward project. The *Driftwood* panel (Fig 9.16) had been drafted on square grid, and looked simple to make but had quirks that led to significant changes in my approach to future patterns.

Derived originally from a piece of marine ply found floating in the sea, a print (Fig 9.15) was made on hospital tissue (which accepts fine detail). The ink on the roller used to prepare the panel had itself been imprinted with the grain of the wood and when this was rolled off, a repeating pattern resulted (Fig 9.13).

The full print was too detailed for complete interpretation, so an interesting section was enlarged and gridded. Several large areas of whole-stitch or half-stitch looked inclined to dominate, so these were shaded by *switching from one stitch to the other* along a dividing line drawn over the pattern. This proved to be the key to unusual effects that I had seen, and admired but never formerly understood, in other modern laces such as that created by Leni Matthaei.

In one area, a number of narrow trails in the design moved too close together for interpretation in the normal Torchon manner which leaves a gap between motifs, so these trails were drawn adjacent with no space. Making this up proved to be possible *if the threads were allowed to interweave between trails* (Fig 9.14). This frees the Torchon technique from the straitjacket imposed by traditional design (as explained on page 125) and encourages more rule-breaking.

The roller print also leads to the design of the *Woodgrain* scarf pattern (page 64), in which a small section of the panel has been repeated in alternating orientations, from both sides of the tracing paper. Only a small amount of alteration had to be done to ensure that the right number of trails flow smoothly from one repeat to the next.

Abstracted strips from this panel have been used for colour-play workshops which have encouraged students to strike out on their own. Several of these may be downloaded from www.contemporarylace.com.

> **Bending lace technique to interpret a natural pattern, instead of adapting the pattern to normal lace processes, was the key to progress here.**

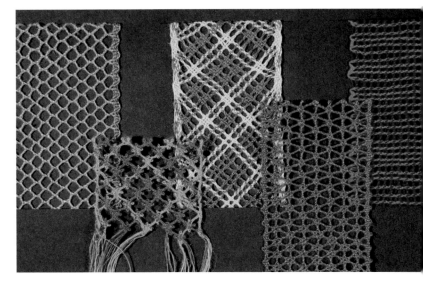

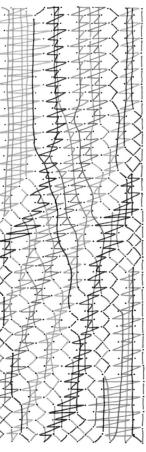

Fig 9.12 *Top: Stitches from Le Puy Enlarged and interpreted in linen 16/2 and 16/1*

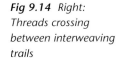

Fig 9.14 *Right: Threads crossing between interweaving trails*

Fig 9.13 *Bottom, left: Roller print after inking wood panel*

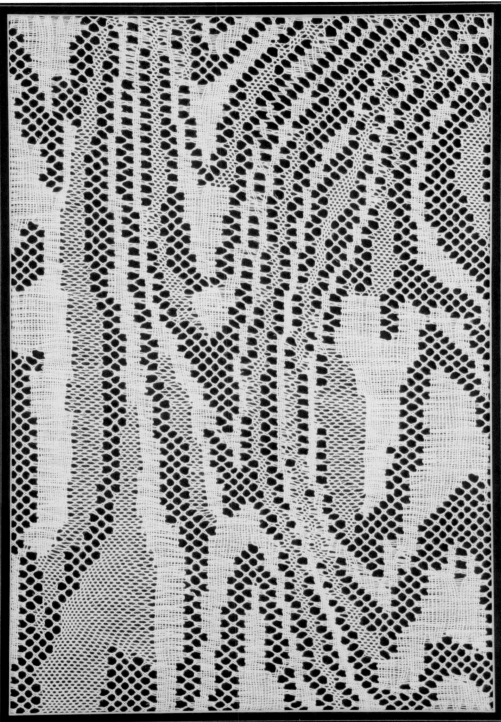

Fig 9.15 *Above:*
Printed driftwood
panel

Fig 9.16 *Right:*
Driftwood, 1994
Linen 16/2
56 x 38 cm

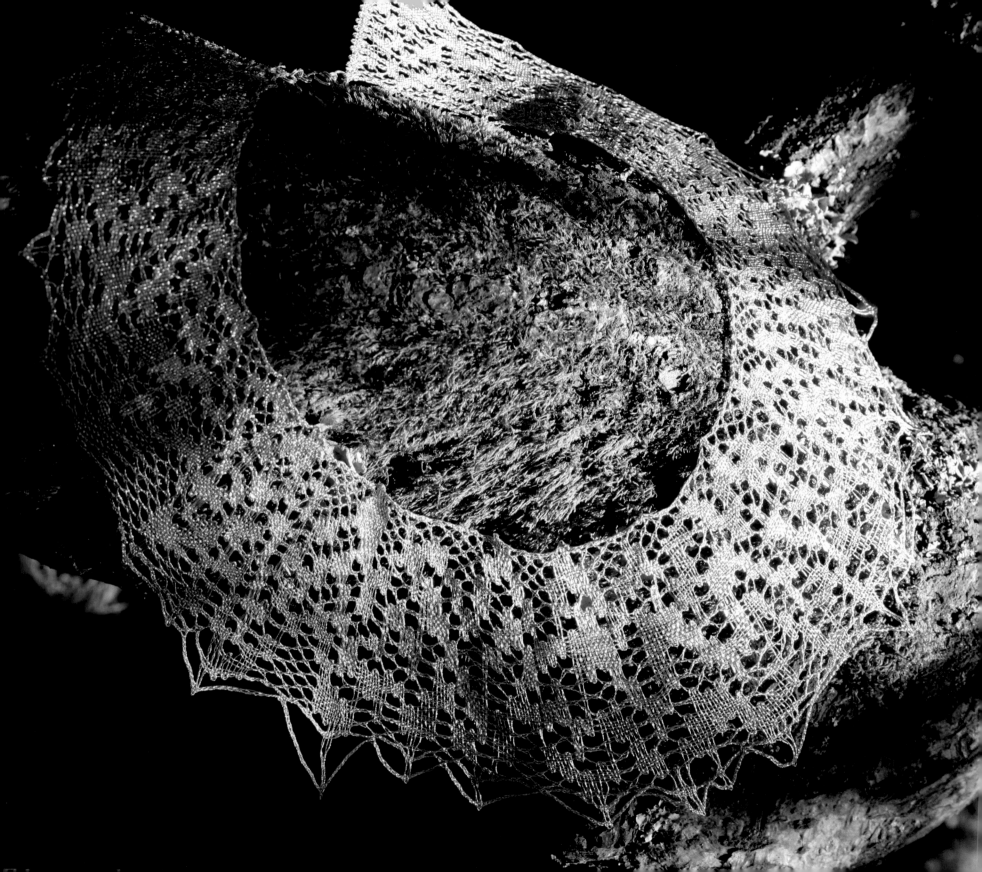

Going with the flow

Once confidence in design starts to grow, pattern possibilities reveal themselves in all kinds of unlikely places. Eyebrows might rise when photos of drainage gratings or unusual door treatments are displayed after an exotic holiday, but once you become a designer you notice patterns everywhere.

The folder illustrated here (Fig 9.18) has travelled with me over many years so now shows signs of hard wear, but the holographic cover begged to be explored. The initial step was to photocopy the back and the front (Fig 9.19); each reproduced a different part of the design (which taught me that holographic designs photocopy differently depending on their orientation). Building up the shapes from the available information, it was found that they fitted quite neatly onto a polar grid (Fig 9.20); such fortuitous discoveries only come from a philosophy of 'leaving no stone unturned' when searching for design sources.

With all the trails spaced in the usual Torchon manner, the circular design allowed just enough detail to achieve the desired effect. The hologram pattern was then lifted dot for dot onto a necklace grid for interpretation with workers in a variety of silver threads which were chosen in contrasting textures (Fig 9.17). The main passives are Madeira metallic no.15, which is a strong and attractive yarn that works well in many different situations.

The edges were developed beyond the limits of the grid, but the necklace was lighter than expected and would sit better if the points had also been beaded. Beautiful crystals, available from Swarovski, could be used for embellishment with spectacular effect.

The circular *Hologram* pattern can be made in many ways, for colour or texture, and could also be enlarged as a tablecloth or redrawn as an edging. Patterns as versatile as this are a treat for a designer since they are inspiring to explore and exciting to make.

Keep your eyes open for anything that might be useful for design work – you just never know what might turn up.

Fig 9.17 Main photo: Hologram *necklace, 2005*
Madeira metallic 15, with other contrasting metallic embroidery threads
31 x 25 cm

Fig 9.18 Above: *Ring binder, WH Smith*

Fig 9.19 Below: *Photocopy of cover*

Fig 9.20 Below right: *Detail from circular hologram pattern*

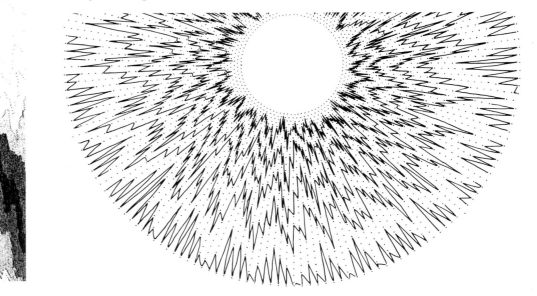

Painting with the computer

The desktop computer is a useful tool for creating patterns that are intriguing to look at but hard to record. Water swirling and eddying in the sea, or down the plughole, proved difficult to draw, paint or photograph but it was possible to create a useful image on the computer.

In the early days, graphic or paint software contained features that had little obvious use; they were there just out of technical innovation. CricketPaint, the program used here, contained a 'barrel distort' function which could be used to pick up part of the screen and swirl it around. About 20 minutes' play with three colours produced an image that had long been on my 'wanted' list but which had hitherto escaped me (Fig 9.22).

Since my printer was not a sophisticated one at that time, the image somehow became distorted, so that the shape explored for lace became slightly elliptical but nonetheless acceptable. It was then enlarged on the photocopier to A2 size.

The process used to grid the pattern was the one detailed on page 46, where two layers of diagonal grid were drawn to accommodate to the image. However, the complicated nature of the centre tended to focus the grid inwards and I discovered that the middle had become considerably denser than the outer area.

The answer proved to be tracing off the centre only, and enlarging that, which then suited the yarn I wanted to try. The pattern is therefore a distorted shape (Fig 9.23), but the final piece has been framed as a rectangle (Fig 9.21).

The same design source was also transferred to polar grid, and the pattern was enlarged to A2 before being made up (see page 54). The thread used, Anchor linen, came in three natural shades, which were used to enhance the effect of the pattern by adding paler shades where needed to emphasise the design.

These days, software has matured and become more task-focused (and less experimental) but it is still possible to create interesting effects with filters or free 'plug-ins' such as Perspective Effects. Some programs intended for 'morphing' faces can also be fun to play with.

Many textile artists are now making extensive use of the computer in their design processes. The tools offered in paint packages can be invaluable in rendering a scanned or photographed image more suitable for design, by simplifying or enhancing various features with commands such as 'twirl', 'cutout' and 'find edges'.

Some graphic design books come with royalty-free patterns on DVD for use with packages such as Adobe Illustrator, Photoshop, Freehand and CorelDraw.

There are also intriguing programs that allow you to play with images: try Gérard Bousquet's SeamlessMaker, from www.hypatisoft.fr, which offers spiral and mandala effects, among others.

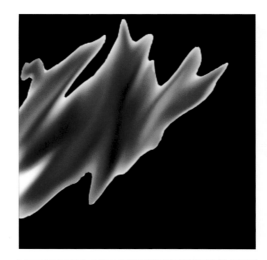

Fig 9.21 Main photo:
Compuswirl I, 1996
Vuorelman linen tow 8
54 x 33 cm
Winner of Founder
Students Trophy,
Lace Guild Reflections
Exhibition 1998

Figs 9.22 Small photos:
Stages in the distortion
process

Fig 9.23 Far right:
The pattern

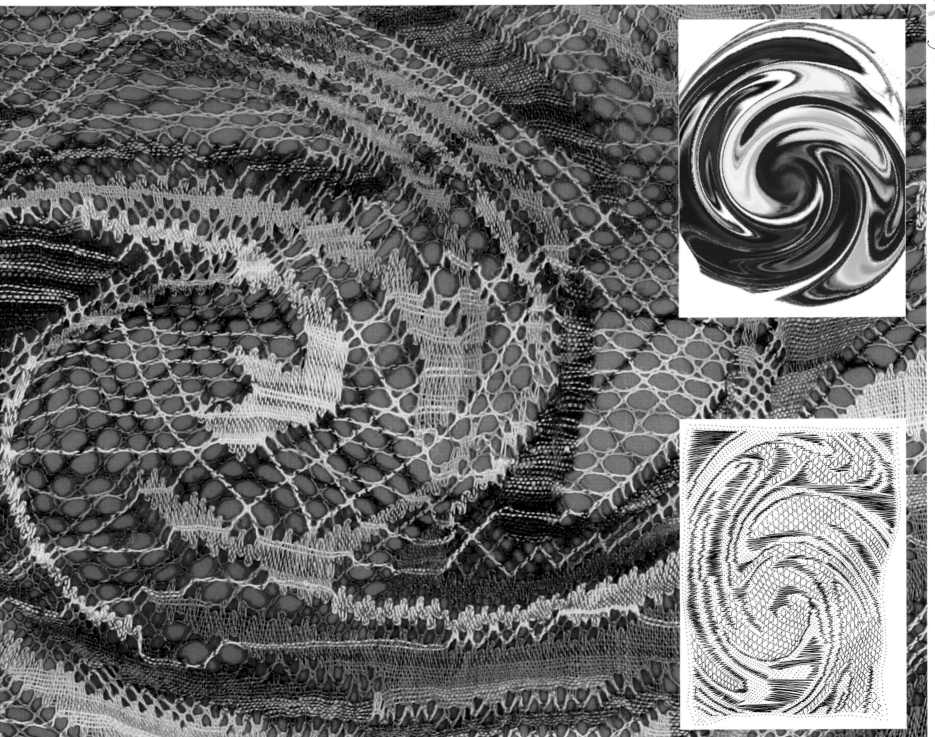

Drawing: trick or treat?

Although we do not have to be able to draw in order to design, it certainly helps. Many people think they cannot do it, but it is a skill that can be learnt with practice rather than being a natural talent accorded to the few.

There are many easy ways to overcome problems. Books such as those by Betty Edwards, or adult education drawing classes and art club life classes, can be of tremendous help for those who feel uncertain. A tutor in one of my life classes suggested that learning to draw was learning to *see*, and spending a few minutes each day drawing everyday objects around the house can quickly boost our confidence.

But then, we can always 'cheat'!

A few years ago the artist David Hockney noticed, at an exhibition of portraits by a major 19th-century French painter, that the heads and the bodies seemed slightly out of proportion. This led him on the intriguing trail of the secret practices used by Old Masters during the previous 400 years, which involved the use of lenses to capture verisimilitude. One had undoubtedly been used during the drawing of the portrait faces, with the bodies added later by eye.

Similar optical devices can still be bought today. The *camera lucida* (Fig 9.24) uses an eye-level prism to project an ethereal image onto drawing paper. The task is then simply to trace it, which takes a small amount of practice, mainly in positioning the source material and in noting registration points that can be referred to if the image shifts because the artist changes position.

This technique places a limit on the drawing size, but it is far, far easier than what Hockney calls 'eyeballing', or drawing by eye alone. Why not treat yourself to a camera lucida?

The two drawings shown here are details from the first and last of three half-hour test-drawing sessions. The first is a leaf from a spray of ivy drawn by eye (Fig 9.25) and the second is a leaf from another spray drawn using the camera lucida (Fig 9.26), after the process had been practised in the second session. The first session felt full of tension, the third felt utterly relaxed.

Another method of creating artwork easily is to trace the image projected onto a wall from a slide. The 35 mm slide is disappearing as digital photography takes over from film but digital projectors are steadily becoming cheaper and more ubiquitous. You just need to fix a large sheet of paper on the wall and trace off details which you may not have had time to include while drawing on-site.

The *Stoneface* design was produced in this way (Fig 9.27). It was gridded for Torchon but the fissures in the rock were interpreted by laying in thicker threads as gimps. When one pair needed to start in the centre of a half-stitch area, the threads were embroidered in before being wound onto bobbins at a more stable point in the lace (Fig 9.28).

If lace design itself is to progress, the ultimate goal should be for projects to develop from original source material. Skill in drawing and design will grow from persistence and determination, and learning to draw is a great confidence-booster. The act of putting pencil to paper sets a mark that can be gauged, evaluated, changed, related, accrued, replaced, moved, attenuated and developed. Don't think about it any further; just do it and then you have something in front of you to edit and improve.

Fig 9.24 Left: *Camera lucida in use*

Fig 9.25 Below: *Leaf tentatively drawn by eye*

Fig 9.26 Left: Confident result using a camera lucida

Fig 9.27 Above: Slide of cliffs at Seacombe Ledge, Isle of Purbeck, Dorset

Fig 9.28 Main photo: Stoneface, 1997 Industrial linen, Texere 128 x 38 cm

121

Fig 9.29 Main photo:
Rust *scarf, 1996*
Linen tow 4 and
knitting yarns, mostly
cotton
180 x 23 cm
Inspiration: rust marks
on the back of a flake
of paint

Insets:
Fig 9.30 Far left:
Rust design work in
Magic Marker

Fig 9.31 Left:
Rust flake

Fig 9.32 Below far
left:
Reuben bread with
acetate tracing (www.
rotellasbakery.com)

Fig 9.33 Below left:
Shapes traced from the
bread

Fig 9.34 Below:
Reuben, 2007
Moravia 50/4 and
40/2 linen
49 cm diameter
First pub: Lace Express

Simple strategies

There are other simple ways of turning inspiration into design; we can doodle with Magic Markers or use our scanner.

Markers are labelled in shades of cool and warm greys which can be used to delineate areas intended for shading with different stitches, different colours, or just different thicknesses of the same thread (Fig 9.30). We can design at a large scale and hang the results up, walk away and evaluate from a distance. Bleed-proof marker paper, like layout paper, is thin enough to see through so that the successful parts can be copied and the less desirable changed.

The *Rust* pattern (Fig 9.29) is very simple, and the colour shading comes about naturally because the vertical patterning prevents threads from either side from mixing. However, other versions have been made in plain colours that focus on texture, both with thread mixtures and with one thread used with different stitches.

Exceptional circumstances suggest different solutions. A slice of marbled Reuben bread (Fig 9.32) from Rotella's Italian Bakery of Omaha, Nebraska, looked too good to eat … The slice was an interesting swirl of colour and texture, with holes in the bread as well as shading in the rye mixture. So the best way to capture the pattern on it was to scan it and email the scan home!

The scan was traced (Fig 9.33) and the shapes were manipulated to arrange them into a more attractive orientation before the pattern was finalised on polar grid. It was then enlarged to A2.

The result could be interpreted in many ways; it might be preferable with one colour and more attention to stitch variation. However, the version illustrated (Fig 9.34) seemed worth trying, although the colours would have been better if a closer blend had been possible in the chosen thread.

The motif colours were added into the ground and hung out again when complete. Towards the centre these were the finer of the two threads since the grid was more cramped. At the finish of each motif the ends were doubled back into the work before being secured by the outgoing passives.

Working with extra threads in Torchon takes a little extra care. There will be one too many passives, until the extra worker is removed.

We can all add our own experiences to problem solving for lace design. Other cultures, art movements and media can all broaden our experience and help develop our personal perspective.

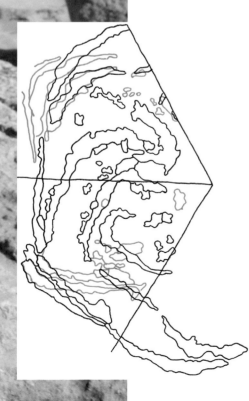

Going it Alone

New rules for old

Traditional laces come with narrowly defined sets of rules and techniques which govern the uniform and optimum production of various styles. With contemporary work we learn to use those that are useful, disregard any that get in the way and make up new ones where needed.

This page looks at some useful tips to overcome problems. For example, a new pair may need to be swiftly added into a scarf, and there are simple ways of avoiding confusion when several trails work side by side. Books that look at practical skills in a general manner (see page 139) help circumvent most problems, but truly personal and innovative work may need to rely on our own ingenuity.

Fig 10.1 Left:
Influenced by Adam
1999
Outer Bockens 40/2;
inner Pella 70, trails
Anchor linen
28 cm diameter
First pub: Lace Express

Knotting in new pairs

Traditional lace methods condition us to avoid knots, but one learns to be more relaxed about them in contemporary work. However, only being able to wind a limited amount of thick thread onto a bobbin may mean we run out of thread earlier than we might have liked, and such thread can be expensive, so we need to think quite carefully when we set up a large piece.

Winding on too much would be wasteful, while too little would cause avoidable knots; getting it right is a matter of experience.

The scarf on page 56 used one cone of silk, with five 'arm's-lengths' of silk on each bobbin and three on the 'selvedges'. Only a few of the threads ran out before the end (my scarves are usually 5 ft long).

Some bobbins do a lot of work and run out quickly, and some meander quietly as passives and remain fairly full. If you do have to add in extra thread, a good place to bury a knot is at a pin in cloth stitch. This is a quick way to do it:

1 Work to the last trail pinhole you can manage.
2 Hang a new pair over the pin so that the two short threads are either side of one new one and knot the short ones around it (Fig 10.2).
3 Weave a couple of stitches with the short threads and hang them out.
4 Weave across with the new ones, and when you have done a couple of rows, pull up and cut off the old threads flush with the work.

Fig 10.2 Knotting in a new pair

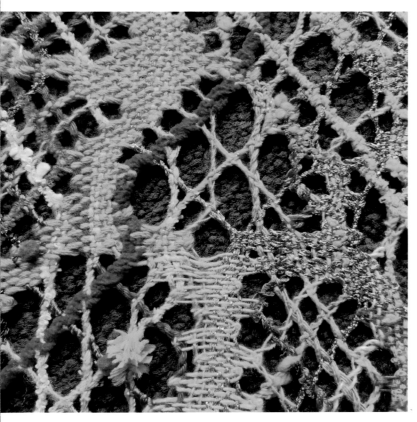

How to avoid confusion when weaving two trails side by side

Torchon is made with two pairs of threads per pinhole (unless another pair has been added in as a different-coloured trail). So whatever game we might play with the pattern or the grid, the number of pairs needed in any particular place is well defined:

- two pairs per pinhole
- four pairs for a two-pin trail
- six pairs for a trail drawn across three pinholes
- eight pairs for a four-pin trail

and so on.

Fig 10.3 *Left: Dancing Water scarf, detail*

Fig 10.4 *Right: A complicated joining point – just count the pinholes*

In a complicated piece of lace, where trails are being divided or joined, it may be difficult to decide how many pairs to take one way and how many the other. There is a simple way to deal with this. Referring to the previous paragraph:

- Just count the pinholes that would be there according to the grid used (Figs 10.3, 10.4).
- Count all the pairs being used, not forgetting the worker pairs from other trails joining at the edges.

The way that passive pairs meander through such work will soon be understood.

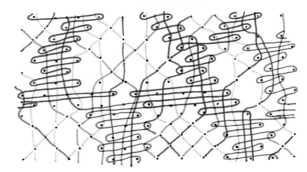

Fig 10.5 *Below: Dividing and joining diagram, from* Influenced by Adam

Dividing and joining trails

When trails join, one worker becomes a passive. When trails divide, one passive becomes a worker. There are various ways of doing this but the thread diagram from one of the polar patterns on page 31 shows how it can be done elegantly (Figs 10.5 and 10.1). The most important thing is to be consistent.

It is more difficult to calculate how to divide trails for patterns on unusual grids if there is no consistent way of working out the number of pinholes involved. Joining is easy: you just incorporate all the available pairs. Again, we have to trust our judgement and unpick it if we have made the wrong decision (or adjust by adding and subtracting bobbins).

Doubling or plying thread

To work with two strands of the same thread on one pair of bobbins:

1 Pull two bobbins-worth of thread from the reel.
2 Double the thread back (so you are now handling two strands at once).
3 Measure off half the length you pulled out to begin with, and wind that doubled thread onto your first bobbin.
4 Use the remaining length of the original thread to measure off the final amount.
5 Cut the thread from the reel and wind the doubled thread onto the second bobbin.

The admonitory lace teacher

Those who have made traditional lace for some time, and know the 'right' way to do things, may find it hard to put aside past experience and do things differently. The 'lace teacher' inside our heads may insist that a certain number of twists should be added here, or a particular stitch there, even though the circumstance alters the case (and if you are self-taught, that voice may be your own!).

Whether we have the courage to disregard convention, or solve the problem using traditional rules, trusting our own judgement is the key to independence. In the end, if you like what you are doing, then it has to be right.

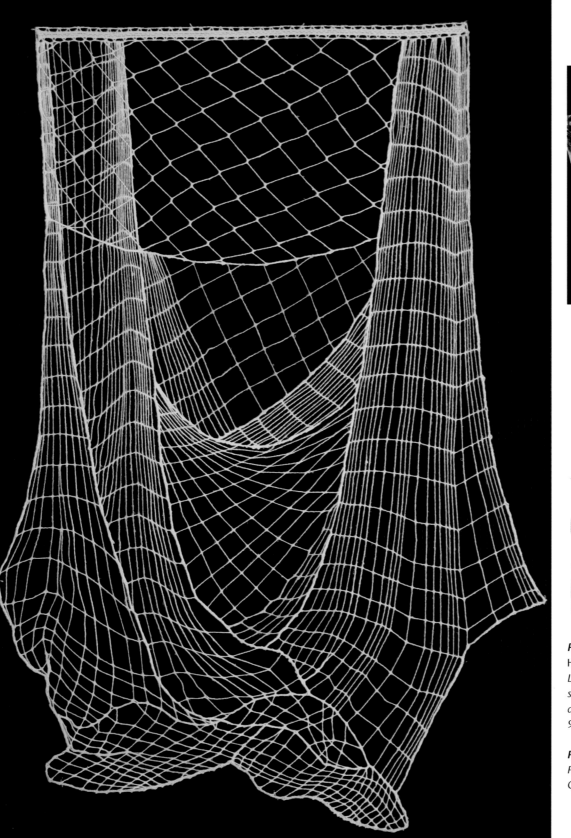

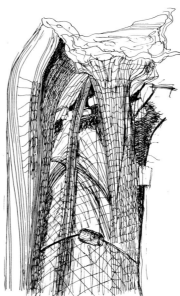

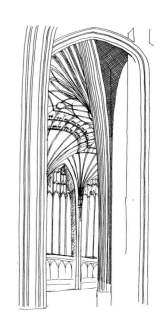

Fig 10.6 Left:
High and Dry, 1994
Linen 16/2 in three
shades, with fine wire
at edge
90 x 60 cm

Fig 10.7 Top:
Fishing nets, Avon
Quay, Mudeford

Fig 10.8 Above left:
Nets explored upside
down

Fig 10.9 Above right:
Vaulting in
Peterborough
Cathedral, which has
shapes strongly related
to the fishing nets

Fig 10.10 Above:
Study for one of
Gaudí's buildings,
recreated in the
museum beneath the
Sagrada Familia

Seeing past obstructions

Complicated-looking problems often have simple solutions. If we have been working for some time on a project without 'seeing the light', it can be useful to have some extra solutions on which to draw.

Do not be put off when you hit a brick wall:

- To thine own self be true.
- Keep your focus.
- Try many different solutions.
- Ask an expert for some clear-sighted appraisal.
- Change long-observed practices.
- Tell someone who you know has your best interests at heart, like your Mum; talking may simplify and solve the problem.
- Change your perspective; turn the work upside down or hold it in front of a mirror.
- Start again.
- Avoid value judgements. Make a list of the qualities you find in your work (elegant, flowing, textured, organic, smooth, contrasting, lively, dynamic, bold, subtle, peaceful, balanced ...) and consider improving weaker points.

Some projects need to go through a number of stages between the stimulus and its resolution. An example of this was *High and Dry* (Fig 10.6), which was inspired by fishing nets at my local quay (Fig 10.7). I was exploring the nets as part of a wider examination of 'structure' at a time when the call for entries went out for a lace competition entitled *The Sensitive Thread*. To what could a thread be sensitive? Perhaps being blown by the wind, the flow of water or, as in the case of the fishing nets, pulled by gravity? This created a fascination with natural forces that never went away.

At the time, I drew the shapes, draped them very simply in string, cut them out in paper, drew some upside down and made them in lace, but there seemed no satisfying way to interpret the nets.

As part of my research into the related shapes of Gothic and neo-Gothic architecture, I considered the work of Antoní Gaudí in Barcelona, because his buildings involve unusual hyperbolic and parabolic arches – Gothic but with rounded tops. These are similar in shape, although not in orientation, to the gravity-pulled catenary into which rope, wire cables or string falls when hung between two points.

I later resolved the work in large scale (90 x 60 cm) in order to create a strong presence for lace in a mixed crafts exhibition. Exploring the net shapes over the full depth of my architect's drawing board was really difficult because I could not judge the bend of the curves I was trying to draw. My 'light-bulb' moment was draping a piece of string down the tilted board, allowing it to form its catenary, and then drawing along beside it. The whole design for *High and Dry* was drawn in this way.

It was 60 cm / 2 ft wide, at a time when my largest pillow had a 46 cm / 18 in. working surface. Therefore the pattern was designed in two sections to be worked independently, with the first section sewn in as the second was made. The piece was stabilised by the vigorous twisting of the vertical pairs (perhaps 15 twists in deep sections) and the outer-edge plait was worked with one pair in fine steel wire, before the completed piece was tied to a wire background.

Some time after this I discovered that Gaudí had created his own designs in a similar manner by draping wires from his studio ceiling, weighting them with little bags of lead shot and then inverting a photograph.

Where to begin/how to end

A useful skill to acquire is the ability to work out how many pairs are needed in a new piece of work. This is vital if you are to become self-sufficient, and will set you up to tackle your own patterns as well as other people's.

Starting

In many pieces, such as *Gothic Tray* (Fig 10.15), it will be necessary to sew the ends back into the beginning. The secret is to find a place where we can start as much as possible on the diagonal edges of a whole-stitch motif, which might involve taking a dog-leg around a pattern.

If we have to start across a trail, it can be advantageous to hang the pairs on a pin laid across the work so we have tiny loops to join into at the end. Count the dots; where crossing trails, work out how many dots there would have been if the grid had continued. Add one pair per diagonal pin; two on each pin across straight grid; extra for the head and foot-side – and wind up what you think you will need. More can always be added.

Study the thread diagram for the piece illustrated to see these instructions in action (Fig 10.11). Drawing the original grid back in over the design shows

that three threads are actually needed between each diagonal pin here, as the steeply slanted Gothic design shape jumps an extra pinhole at each step.

Pattern diagrams in other lace books can also be studied as generic rather than specific demonstrations. You can ask yourself 'what would I do here?' and then see if you were right. Torchon is a very straightforward lace because there are always two pairs per pin once the work is in progress and starting is just a question of ensuring that we have this number in place.

It is always worthwhile unpicking the work if something is seriously amiss. The start sections of some of the early pieces in this book were unpicked a number of times, for instance when colours did not look good together.

Finishing

Neat ways of joining work together on the pillow are particularly useful when working with delicate threads. There are some excellent books that can help, including Bridget Cook's *Practical Skills in Bobbin Lace*, which was used to find the correct joining method for silk work, such as *Gothic Tray* (Fig 10.15).

The tray was photographed to show the lace design, but in holding it up to

the light, a dominant feature has become the join. This has been rolled and sewn with a very fine silk thread, which is invisible from the front (Fig 10.13) and neat at the back (Fig 10.14) under normal conditions. It seemed safest to finish the floss silk lace while it was protected by being pinned out to shape.

For ordinary work a fail-safe method is to sew the ends down into the final knot and back up through the knot again. Cut them off flush when all the threads have been secured. Threads can be cut in half after being sewn in, to show which have been completed.

Some pieces in this book have been started and finished into a plait in the Czech manner; an easy place to find this method is in one of Jana Novak's *Moravia* books; an outline of the technique follows:

1 Starting on a plait (see Fig 2.8 for an example) involves hanging a new pair over one thread of the plait.
2 At the finish, pairs are taken out through a plait in whole-stitch.
3 The two central threads of the plait are then hung out.
4 The plait continues on to incorporate the next pair. For extra security, a knot can be buried in the process, and invisible oversewing added.

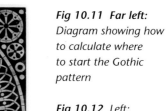

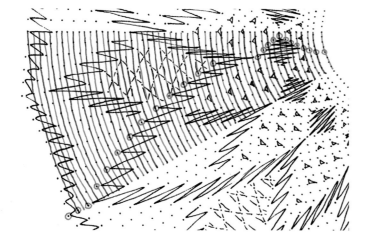

Fig 10.11 Far left: Diagram showing how to calculate where to start the Gothic pattern

Fig 10.12 Left: A Gothic pavement inspired the tray

Fig 10.13 Top: Join from front

Fig 10.14 Above: Join from back

Fig 10.15 Main photo: Gothic Tray, 1989 Piper 300/4 silk floss, with 800 floss in the trail and 600 at the edge 36 cm diameter

Finishing

If you are used to handling traditional lace in a delicate manner, then the finishing techniques of other textiles may come as a shock. Commercial silk scarves might be swirled through jets of hot water, to enhance gloss and drape, and linen may be boiled and beetled (crushed) with a roller, to create a shining surface. It is said that woollen cloths are made in the finishing: fulling or milling wool at home could mean trampling a piece of cloth in warm soapy water for several hours in order to create a hard-wearing result.

When first experimenting with scarves, the initial temptation was to put them away in a drawer protected in tissue, but they really do have to stand up to normal wear. If you make a scarf in high-quality yarn and finish it properly, you should be able to use it for years to come.

Ironing

Woven silk scarves can be washed and ironed dry and so can lace ones. When first off the pillow the lace may look unremarkable, and washing may reduce it to a dish-rag. However, steam-ironing it dry, moving the iron along to polish the silk, produces a quite different fabric. It is heavy, glossy and drapes beautifully, just like a Jermyn Street product. The silk scarf on page 56 has been finished in this way.

Blocking

Blocking involves stretching a textile out to its full size, wetting it and leaving it to dry. It will then retain its shape. Some pieces, such as knitted woollen Shetland shawls, only attain their full beauty in this way. All fibres respond to blocking. It is especially helpful for wool but linen also responds well, stiffening if left to dry naturally, and it is also good for silk.

Scarves that contain stretchy yarns such as those designed for knitting will shrink when they come off the pillow, but blocking stretches them back. The scarf shown here (Fig 10.16) was originally 55 cm wide, shrank by about 20%, but is only 10% narrower after blocking.

A 6 ft piece of softboard covered with plastic is ideal for blocking scarves. Mark out the original size of the pattern, and pin the lace to this, with a pin in each of the edge pinholes. Since this process returns the lace to its original tension the pins need to be strong. The process will also take some time. Then spray or paint the lace with clean water so that it is sodden, and leave it to dry naturally before removing the pins. I keep blocking pins separately and check for rust before using them again.

Washing yarn

Linen tow weaving yarns that come in skeins will soften if washed before use, and also soften with blocking. To wash the yarn, open it out, re-skein and tie it with figure-of-eight ties in several places. Soak for half an hour in liquid soap; rinse carefully, dry and ball. This also removes many of the loose fibres.

Mangling or beetling

Linen can also be mangled. Few people still possess an old mangle, but two chopping boards and a rolling-pin will do the job. Wet the item, place it on top of one of the boards, place the rolling-pin on top and use the second board to roll the pin back and forth, pressing down as you do it. This will flatten the fibres. Woven linen tow tablecloths that have been mangled look smooth and lustrous. Steam-iron the item to dry it, or block it and leave it to dry naturally.

It is good to try out on a sample first any finishes that may change the nature of the item, in case you do not like the result. One half of a sample for *Betula*, page 108, was mangled, and it changed considerably, so the decision was made to only block the finished item (Figs 10.17 and 10.18).

Stiffening

Although all stiffening solutions change the lustre of the component threads, stiffening might be necessary with a 3D piece. Powertex, used to stiffen textiles, can also be bought with an optional additive for outdoor use.

Fringes

Well over fifteen years have now passed since I made my first scarf, and most of those illustrated in this book have been worn from time to time. This has shown that my initial idea of knotting the ends as tassels can be vulnerable to wear and tear. Plied knitting and embroidery threads containing rayon and metallic filaments can tangle in normal wear.

I currently make plaited fringes, and there are other ideas yet to be explored. Knotting was used for tablemats (Fig 5.15), and various methods of twisting look promising.

Plaits will need to be knotted at both ends; at least 23 cm / 9 in. of plait are required for a 15 cm / 6 in. fringe.

Start a scarf by plaiting two pairs together, tie an overhand knot when the plait is long enough and skewer the knot to the first pinhole of the work. Repeat with each starting pin.

On completing the scarf, plait the remaining threads as long as required and cut and knot each plait to prevent it unravelling. Go back to the bottom of the scarf and knot each plait around the last pin. Lay a piece of tape across 15 cm below the last pins (or as required) and re-knot and cut the ends of the plaits to a uniform length along the tape. Re-pin the top of the scarf and finish the plaits to match (Fig 10.19).

Unplaited free-thread fringes can be

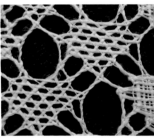

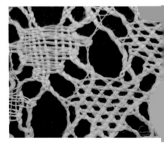

Fig 10.16 Top: Leopard spot *scarf*, 2008
50% linen tow 4, 50% knitting yarns
In the process of being blocked; pins removed, it was 8 cm / 3 in. wider than an unblocked version

looped and knotted at the start and cut off at the end, leaving plenty of spare thread. This thread should be wetted and ironed until straight, before trimming, to remove the kinks left after threads have been wound onto bobbins. To cut the fringe, comb out the threads, lay a straight edge across the ends and trim them. Complete both ends of the scarf to match.

One experiment was to knot and bead the ends of *Dancing Water* (page 97) in various ways. No two-pair component was finished like another. They made use of large and small beads and a variety of knotting patterns and some ends were left fairly free. This was too complicated – simple methods of finishing stand up best to hard wear.

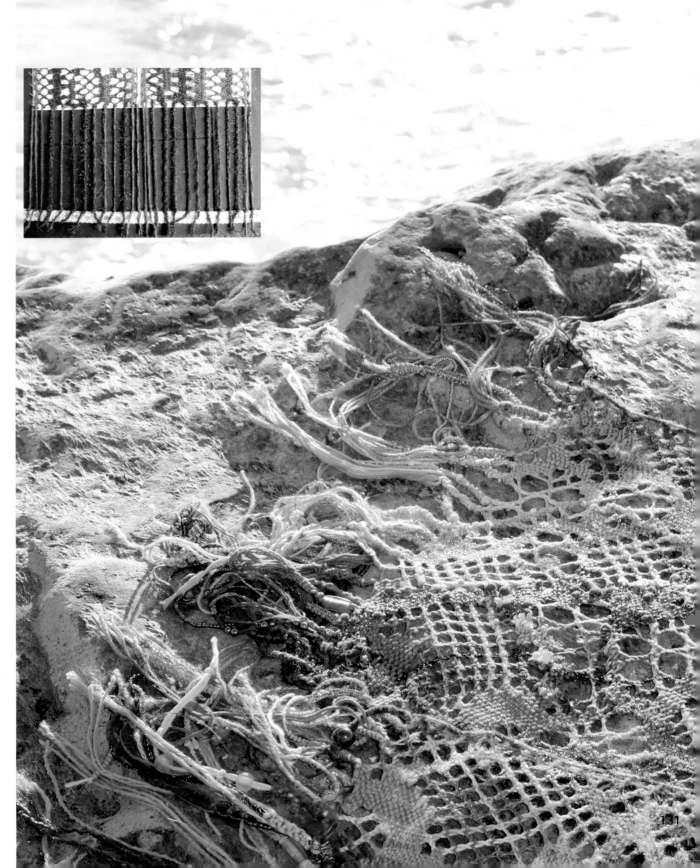

Hanging bars

It seems best to sew lace onto a hanging bar after its completion, as experience has shown that knotting threads onto bars before starting the work can bring problems.

One top thread of a lightly exhibited hanging, which had been knotted around its hanging bar, snapped in storage. In another case, the top bar of a hanging posted abroad was broken in transit. There is no way back from this; it proved impossible to insert a new bar into the loops of the lark's head knots from which it had been started.

If using an acrylic bar, fishing line or strong thread may be used to attach the lace. If anything goes wrong, simply untie the lace and start again.

Fig 10.17 *Centre left:* Betula *sample off the pillow*

Fig 10.18 *Bottom left:* Betula *sample after mangling*

Fig 10.19 *Inset above right:* *Plaiting fringes to match scarf ends*

Fig 10.20 *Right:* *Fringe of* Dancing Water *scarf*

Resources

Equipment

Some of the work in this book has been made with traditional equipment, but much has needed bespoke pillows and bobbins. The market constantly changes, so the information given here, and in the list on page 139, highlights the best of what is available at the time of writing.

New equipment need not be expensive; it is even possible to make it yourself. For example, pillows can be made from blocks of polystyrene insulation available from DIY stores, and bobbins whittled from thick dowelling.

Pillows

The largest off-the-peg pillows are a good start, but it is also possible to make large pieces of lace by resting a piece of insulation board on a table, propping it against a wall or even sitting astride it. Personal experience suggests that Styrofoam blocks are preferable to polystyrene.

However, the extra cost of commissioning a large-scale pillow would never be regretted and if one is making lace for long periods it is important to sit with a good posture, the pillow tilted and the shoulders and arms relaxed.

Pillow makers usually respond positively to special commissions. Plans shown in Fig 11.2 are both for Styrofoam pillows: (a) 91 cm / 3 ft diameter with nine 15 cm / 6 in. square blocks and

(b) 132 cm / 52 in. wide with eight 49 cm / 18 in. x 11 cm / 4.5 in. bars. Although they store flat against the wall, the problem is finding suitable space in which to use them and they severely restrict one's ability to attend pillow-parties!

Making large pieces of lace with many bobbins is a very different operation from Central European techniques using bolster pillows and few bobbins, but Torchon is also made on such pillows, where waiting bobbins are stored behind the lace rather than at the side.

Bobbins

The large Dutch bobbins which I first used when experimenting with thick thread are still available, although these have relatively small heads which do not take large quantities of thick thread. Larger ones are made in Germany and economical ones can be ordered from Prague. Different bobbins suit different projects or certain threads – the plum bobbins in Fig 11.1 are lovely for 16/2 linen, for instance.

As previously mentioned, it is possible to make bobbins at home. Those produced by Shelly Canning have been constructed cheaply on pea-sticks, with handles of rolled corrugated cardboard and cotton balls and heads made from beads. Using wood, a whittling knife from the local hardware store and some lengths of thick dowelling, plus fine

sandpaper, it is possible to produce a usable bobbin in about half an hour. Resourceful lacemakers have also been known to use medical tongue-depressers, dolly-pegs, cut card shapes – and there are, no doubt, many other solutions.

Pins

Large-scale lacemaking needs large pins, and blocking large pieces of work needs strong ones. There is now just one European pin-maker left, in Spain. Folch produce their Jabali lace pins in brass, hard steel and stainless steel, some with nickel plating. Some have glass and plastic heads and heads dipped with different colours. Their extensive website explains the variations, but all their large pins are excellent. Brass 42 mm will suit very large work; steel 45 mm are also good for blocking; 38 mm stainless steel are excellent for general work; and 49 mm glass-headed make good dividers.

Patterns

Traditional patterns were pricked through first, but photocopies laminated with 75 micrometre film need no such preparation, if one uses steel pins. Patterns sandwiched between sticky-back plastic and thin card work well but one-off designs can be worked directly over a paper pattern. If you have problems seeing your lace on white paper, use a colour that suits you better.

Fig 11.1 Main photo: Bobbins collected over many years, left to right: 16 cm Shelly Canning; 13.5 cm Czech, 17 cm Langendorf; 10.5 cm Belgian; 22 cm Czech. Vertical: 20 cm Czech; 12 cm Langendorf plum; 16 cm whittled.

Centre front: 9.5 cm traditional, with whittled dowelling. Centre back: fat 15 cm John Tappenden. Vertical: slimmer 15 cm John Tappenden crossed with 20 cm Czech. Rear: Whittled Slovak; 15 cm

Dutch with whittled dowelling and 10 cm painted dowelling weighted with bead. Rear: Whittling knife. Front: Dolly peg.

Fig 11.2 a, b Plans for large pillows

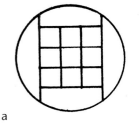

a

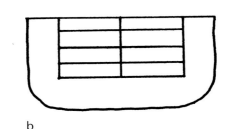

b

Yarns suitable for lace

A wide range of yarns are suitable for bobbin lace if we celebrate the special contribution they can make and work with their limitations – a wealth of yarns are created for embroidery, weaving and knitting but lace can use them, too.

Yarns have been selected for these tables because of special features, including colour-range, stability, reliability and availability. A few foreign yarns

bought abroad have been added to encourage travellers to 'buy and try'.

Fancy knitting yarns change too fast to be included here; they have been used extensively in work in this book, but are often found serendipitously. Using them in conjunction with linen can help to overcome most difficulties which 'effect' yarns might add.

Torchon can be enlarged, reduced or

redrafted to suit most threads; Plotadot grids are now available to match most of the dot-pitches given here.

Information on how to 'Tex' and sample your own threads is given on page 62. The sampling pattern is on page 138. For dot pitches 11 and above, either draft on graph paper or photocopy the 10 mm section at 110%, 120% and so on.

Cottons

Name	Maker/Supplier	DP	Range	Tex	Cols	USP	Other qualities	Problems	Uses	For	Examples
Super American Mercerised Cotton 2/20s	William Hall	5	4–6	50	14	Large spool of quality thread			Excellent basic thread	W	
Special Dentelles	DMC	4	4–6	50	51	Coloured lace thread				L	Fig 3.27
Colcoton 34/2	Claires's Lace	5	4–5	50	113	Good colour range, lustrous		Soft; re-twist constantly to prevent breaking	Good for polar patterns	E	Fig 5.21
Egyptian 2/20s gassed cotton	William Hall	5		55		Economical quality thread for lace				W	
Finca 30	Roseground	5	4–5	60		Good lace thread				L	
SAMC 2/12s	William Hall	7	6–8	120	36	Large spool of quality thread				W	
Pearl cotton 8	DMC	7	6–9	125 (115)	238	Splendid for colour effects	Ball goes a long way		General	E	Fig 3.10
SAMC 2/6s	William Hall	9/10	8–10	200	36	Large spool of quality thread	Similar to pearl cotton but cheaper		Mix into colour schemes	W	Fig 5.6
Stranded cotton	DMC/Anchor etc.	10	9/12	220	Many	Ubiquitous	Precise shades	Short lengths	Colour schemes	E	Many
Pearl cotton 5	DMC	11	10–12	250 (208)	312	Building colour palettes		Less economical than pearl 8		E	Fig 3.67
4-ply cotton	Patons	12	11–13	310	Many	Lustrous sheen			Scarves etc.	K	
4-ply knitting cotton	Many	12	11–13	315	Many	Widely available, fashion colours	Strong, reliable		Scarves etc.	K	
Fine cotton rayon chenille	William Hall (others from Texere etc.)	10	11–14+	340	12	Texture in 16/2 linen projects		Coned – share with friends	Scarves, panels etc.	W	Fig 5.6 (bright red)
Cotton/bamboo DK	Patons Serenity			410	14	Good basic high street DK	Soft		Scarves etc.	K	
Provence DK	Texere	16	15/17	570	Some	Coned, economy			Scarves etc.	K	
Monaco Aran	Texere	210	20/23	675	Some	Coned, economy			Scarves etc.	K	
Coarse round cotton rayon chenille	William Hall	15+		2280		Mix with coarse yarns for texture	Dyes well	Large cone to share	Scarves etc.	W	Fig 7.10 (one of many textures)

Key for thread tables:
Suppliers TB: Theo Brejaart; RSD: Riitta Sinkkonen Davies
W: weaving; L: lace; K: knitting; E: embroidery; S: saddlery; C: craft
Tex number in brackets: spinner's own

Linens

Name	Maker/Supplier	DP mm	Range mm	Tex	Cols	USP	Other qualities	Problems	Uses	For	Examples
Texere Galway x2	Texere	4 6	4–5	30	22	Fine, coloured, quite strong	Good support for problem threads	Best doubled or blended	Infinite	W	
Bockens 60/2	Holma, many lace suppliers	4/5	4–6	45	20	Good lace thread			Can be used for polar pattern	L	Fig 6.5
Linen & steel	Bart Francis	5	4–7	60		Steel supports delicate lace		Small reels		W	
Bockens 40/2	Holma, many lace suppliers	5		70	3	One of 11 thicknesses	Lustrous, reliable, default linen	Natural, ½ bl and bleach only	Many and various	L	Fig 7.4
Czech fine weaving	CZ	5	4–6	70	Many	Hand-dyed, lovely colours	Strong, economical	How to get hold of it!	Infinite	W/L	
Moravia 40/2	Moravia, many lace suppliers	5	5–6	70	46	Good coloured lace linen	Expanding colour range	No 'muddy' colours, soft	Endless, incl. polar pattern	L	Fig 8.12
Vavlin 40/2	Klippans, Zurcher, TB	6	6–7	75	75	Many	soft	Watch and retwist	Many	W, L	Fig 3.27
Bockens Lingarn 16/1	Holma (buy William Hall)	6	5–8+	80	70	Bright colours (a bit hairy)	Versatile, equiv. to 40/2	Re-twist fairly frequently	As above	W	Fig 7.4
Texere Connemara	Texere	7	6–8	80	4	Coloured, very strong	Stiff and stable	Few colours	Household	W	
Bockens 35/2	Holma	5/6	5–7	100	20	Good lace linen	Coloured	Limited colours	Many, incl. polar	L	Fig 10.1
Vuorelma 30/2	RSD	7	7–8	110	4	Strong, soft	Weaving		Household, hangings	W	Fig 2.23
Anchor linen	Anchor	7/8		120	3	Strong, matt	Natural shades	Hard to find UK	Household, hangings	E?	Fig 4.3
Czech linen, thin	CZ	8	7–9	120	Various	Smooth, strong	Colours emerging	Only CZ	Many	L	
Moravia 50/4	Moravia	7	7–8	130	46	Strong coloured thread	Expanding colour range	No 'muddy' colours	Larger-scale pieces	L	Fig 9.34
Polish linen	Bobowa	13	8–13	150	2	Very stiff, strong	Smooth	Only Poland	Endless	L	Fig 2.23
Pella 30	Vuorelma	8		160	3	Tough, smooth	versatile	Availability	Various	L	
Czech linen, med	CZ	13	12–14	170	Various	Smooth, strong	Some colours	Only CZ		L	Fig 2.14
Pella 50/70	Vuorelma	-, 6,		110, 70	3	Lovely thread	Stiff and strong			L	Fig 10.1
Bockens Lingarn16/2	Holma (buy William Hall)	9/10	8–10	190	70	Bright colours, strong, smooth	Versatile, reliable, durable	Colours unsubtle (so use in bright projects)	Hangings, household	W	Fig 8.20 and many others, samples
Vavlin 16/2	Klippans, Zurcher, TB	9/10	8–10	200	75	Bright and subtle colours	Strong, smooth, versatile	Availability	As above	W	Fig 3.58
Goldschildt 30/3, 50/3, 66/3, 80/3	Goldschildt, lace suppliers in EU and USA	7, 6, 5, 5		130, 110, 80, 70	25	Strong, smooth, stiff	Good stable lace thread	Limited colour palette, availability	Wide range of lace projects	L	Fig 8.12
Vuorelma Rhodinlanka linen tow 8	Vuorelma, RSD	10	9–11	(210) 190	62	Bright and subtle colours	Strong, versatile	Hairy (can wash first); single thread so retwist	Practical lace of all kinds	W	Fig 9.21
Barbour 18/3 upholstry	saddlery	10	10–12	270		Very strong	High twist		Large items	S	
Texere C4	Texere	13	11–14	410	33	Thick, coloured	Versatile,	Available for limited time	Hangings etc.	W	
Rhodinlanka linen tow 4	Vuorelma, RSD	14	13–15	(420) 350	62	As no 8, but even stronger	Good to add stability to other yarns	As no 8, will soften in use	Scarves, hangings etc.	W	Fig 4.8 and many others
Texere fine (rug warp)	Texere	15	14–17	510	2	Thick, multi-strand	Very strong and stable	White or cream, smooth or hairy, as available	Hangings etc.	W	Fig 2.1
Texere medium	Texere	18	17–21	580	2	As above, thicker				W	Fig 2.1
Texere thick	Texere	22	++	1110	2	As above, thicker still				W	Fig 2.1
Texere Dublin best twist	Texere	24+	23++	1620	natural	Strong and thick	plied	Bulky – find a use for it!	Something outdoors?	W	

Silks

Name	Maker/Supplier	DP	Range	Tex	Cols	USP	Other qualities	Problems	Uses	For	Examples
Italian silk/steel x1 x2 X3	Danish Yarn Purchasing Assocn, Habu	3 5 7	2–4 4–6 6–8	20	1	Very fine but retains shape	Easy to use on bobbins	Handle with care – once bent, lace cannot be flattened again	Extensive	W	Fig 6.8
Bart Francis Argentina x1 X2 X3 X4	Bart Francis	4 5 6	4–5 4–6 3–7	20	Many	Strong, glossy, superb colours, plies well, very versatile	Luxurious	Availability	Various, incl. polar patterns	E	
De Vere 18	De Vere	4	4–5	30	96	Good choice of colour and sizes	Strong and glossy, two spool sizes	All silk is expensive	Many; luxury gifts	E	
Gütermann 100/3		4	4–5	30	Many	Extensive colour range	Silky sheen	Can snap at knot	Used in art laces	E	Fig 4.11 in mixture
HWC spun silk	Hand Weaving Company	4		30	Various	Large spools, good colours	Economical			W	Fig 4.11 in mixture
Piper 3fold 90 floss	Piper	4		40	235	Extensive colour range	Versatile	Floss needs protecting	Polar and other patterns	E	Fig 10.15 uses 300/4 (old stock)
Bart Francis jaspé silk x1 X2	Bart Francis	6 10	6–7 9–10	60	Various	Texture, character yarn	Strong and resilient	Rough appearance	Texture	W	
Piper 800 floss	Piper			90	235	Extra texture	High gloss	Handle with care	Various, polar	E	Fig 10.15
Texere Silk Heather x1 +linen x2	Texere	NO 8 10	7–10 9–12	100	Various	Soft, slubby, tweedy; only use plied with fine linen or itself	Silk/wool/cotton, with subtle sheen apparent in use, misty colours	Must be plied – good with Galway linen	Various – surprisingly useful for texture work	W/K	
Fine bourette silk	Texere	8	8–9	110	1	Rough silk, cream	Dyes well	Matt – good as contrast to sheen	Wearables	W/K	
William Hall 10/2 spun silk	William Hall	8	7–9	120	1	Pearly lustre			Wearables	W	
Zurcher Tussah x1 X2	Zurcher	8 14	7–9 12–14	125	48	Delightful palette	Strong, lustrous and soft	Matt appearance	Wearables, double for swift scarves	W	Fig 4.11 in mixture
De Vere 72	De Vere	10	10–11	140	96	Good choice of colour and sizes	Strong and glossy, two spool sizes	All silk expensive, handle with care	Luxury gifts	E	
Texere 16/2 spun silk	Texere	9/10	8–11	140	1	Soft and lustrous, good basic thread	Dyes beautifully	All silk is expensive	Wearables	W	Fig 4.16
3-ply bourette silk	Texere	10	9–12	170	1	Rough silk, cream	Dyes well	Matt – good as contrast to sheen	Wearables	W	
Alchemy Silken Straw	Loopknitting.com	10	10–11	180	16	Flat woven dyed yarn, unique	Strong, unusual, goes a long way	Special silk is expensive	Add as special feature	K	Fig 5.27 various
4-ply bourette silk	Texere	12	11–13	240	1	Rough silk, cream	Dyes well	Matt – good as contrast to sheen	Wearables	W	Fig 5.27
Texere 8/2 spun silk	Texere	11	10–12	260	1	Good compromise on price v speed	Dyes beautifully	All silk is expensive	Wearables	W	Fig 4.5
Texere 5/2 spun silk	Texere	14	15+	370	1	Thicker contrast, gimp	Dyes beautifully	All silk is expensive	Wearables	W	Fig 4.16
Thai silk	Texere	13	12–13	370	1	Some sheen, pale toffee colour			Wearables	W/K	Fig 5.27
Texere 2/5/2				780	1	Heavy silk	Contrast with lighter weights	All silk is expensive	Wearables	W	Fig 4.5 selvedge
17/8 bourette silk	Texere	15	14–16	405	1	Rough silk, cream	Dyes well	Matt – good as contrast to sheen	Wearables	W	Fig 5.27

Rayon

Name	Maker/Supplier	DP	Range	Tex	Cols	USP	Other qualities	Problems	Uses	For	Examples
Maltese 300 X2	Malta	10	9–12	110		Maltese make lace with it; why not us?				W	
Folded viscose rayon 1200/2 X1 X2	William Hall	7 12	6–9 11–14	135	48	Adds shine to a mix of threads or use alone	Drape and lustre, lovely colours	'Lively' to control	Many, mix into wearables	W/K	Fig 4.13
FVR 1800/2 bright viscose floss	William Hall	10	9–11	210	1	Add shine to mixed project	Dyes well		Heavyweight projects	W	
Texere viscose floss	Texere	10	8–10	210		Viscose dyes well		Check all viscose for strength		W/K	
Texere viscose ribbon	Texere	14	13–14	310		Viscose dyes well				W/K	

Other threads

Name	Maker/Supplier	DP	Range	Tex	Cols	USP	Other qualities	Problems	Uses	For	Examples
Cashmere	Patricia Roberts	12	11–14		6	Very soft	Quite limp	Expensive	Scarves	K	Fig 4.8
Synthetic raffia	Uppingham yarns	13	12–14	80	Several	Stiff and stable, decorative	Looks like audio tape		Panels, room divider?	?	
Kidsilk Haze x2	Rowan	13	12–16	110x1	29	Soft but not scratchy	Fewer tangles than mohair	Unwind, not unroll, from bobbins	Scarves etc.	K	
Habu ramie	Habu, NY	12	10–14	130		Quite fine but stiff	Capable of delicate statement		Decorative, supportive	W	Fig 4.15
Czech hemp	CZ	9	8–12	180		Add texture to linen, or use alone	Stiff, pliant, slightly rough	Catch it if you can	Decorative	W	Fig 4.1
Banana fibre	Bart Francis	11	10–12	180		Lustrous, stiff, straw-like filament	Good for sculptures, hats	Surprisingly strong	3D	W	
3-strand hemp	Ecolution, Annie Sherburne	12	11–13	310		Stiff but pliant			Hangings?	C	
Dyed kasuri bamboo tape	Habu	25	++	400		Acts like raffia, but in a ball	Suitable for large work		Much potential	C	Fig 4.15
Handspun nettle fibre		18	17–19	410		Heavy texture		Feels like sandpaper!		K	Fig 4.15
6-strand hemp	Ecolution, Annie Sherburne	16	15–17	590		Stiff but pliant				K, C	
Hemp: 4-ply 2-ply Single	House of Hemp	19 12 9	18–20 11–14 8–14	750 340 140	21	Interesting colours, range of sizes or ply yourself	Strong and pliant	Hairy	Hangings and household	W, K	
Handspun banana				1260		Lovely lustre				K	

Patterns for thread sampling

(see page 62)

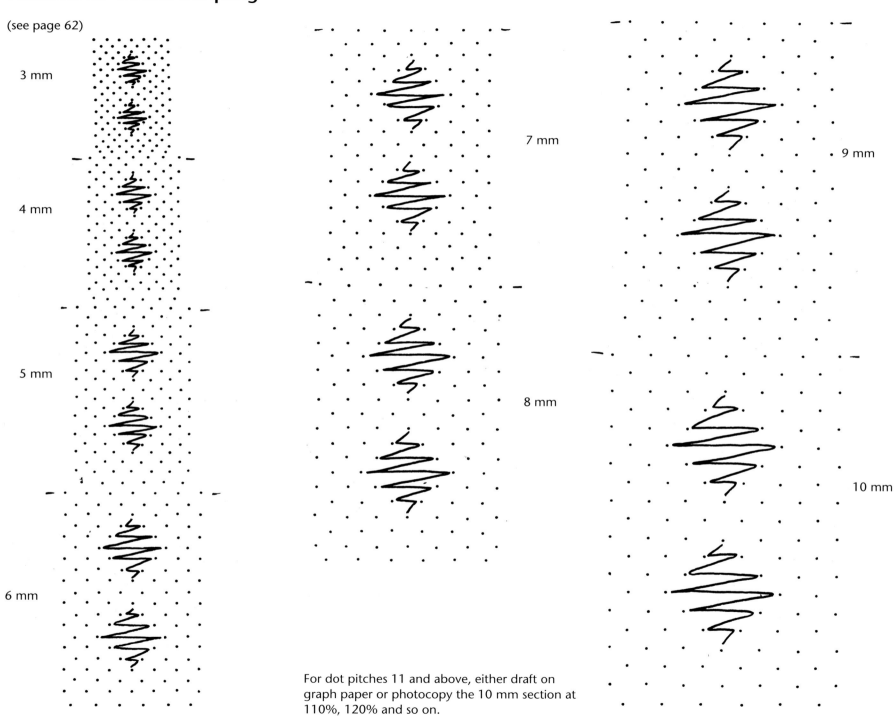

3 mm

4 mm

5 mm

6 mm

7 mm

8 mm

9 mm

10 mm

For dot pitches 11 and above, either draft on
graph paper or photocopy the 10 mm section at
110%, 120% and so on.

Resources

Suppliers

All supplies are subject to constant change.

Yarn

Bart Francis: www.bart-francis.be
De Vere Yarns: www.devereyarns.co.uk
Holly Van Sciver:
www.vansciverbobbinlace.com
Holma-Helsinglands AB: www.holma.se
House of Hemp: www.houseofhemp.co.uk
Klippans: www.klippansyllefabrik.se
Martin Burkhard: www.ateliermb.ch
Moravia: www.ateliermoravia.com
Texere: www.texere.co.uk
Theo Brejaart: www.theobrejaart.nl
Vuorelma in UK: Riitta Sinkkonen Davies;
www.rasdavies.co.uk
Vuorelma: www.vuorelma.net
William Hall: 177 Stanley Road, Cheadle
Hulme, Cheadle, Cheshire SK8 6RF
Zurcher.Stalder AG: Postfach, CH-3422
Kirchberg, Switzerland; email zsag@zsag.ch

Bobbins

Czech bobbins: www.palickovani.cz
Langendorf, Germany:
www.langendorfkloeppel.de
Dutch bobbins: www.clareslace.co.uk

Pillows

www.churchmeadowcrafts.com

Pins

www.folch.com; also via Presencia from
www.bigginslace.co.uk

Grids

Plotadot grids: www.knittedlacefans.com

Patterns in this book

www.contemporarylace.com

Sundries

Acrylic rod: www.modelshop.co.uk
Bags: www.clippykitlondon.co.uk
Camera lucida: www.cameralucida.org.uk
Crystals: www.swarovski-crystallized.com
Findings, clasps: www.kernowcraft.com
Froebel toys: www.froebelusa.com
Indigo: www.vivienprideaux.co.uk
Powertex: www.powertex.be
Tie interfacing: www.macculloch-wallis.co.uk

Inspiration

Lace with light: Sonumbra, www.loop.ph;
fibre optics, www.glofab.se
Exhibitions:
Kantlijnen, Bruges, 2009
McFadden, D R, *Radical Lace and Subversive Knitting*, Museum of Arts and Design, New York, 2007
Museum des Manufactures de Dentelles, *Les Contours du Vide,* Retournac, 2008
Contemporary lace:
www.varenne.pierre.chezalice.fr
www.ghosttreestudio.co.uk
www.carolquarini.com
www.98lacegroup.org.uk
www.westhopegroup.org.uk
www.lenkas.com

Books

Textile techniques

Mangling explained in: Osterkamp, Peggy, *New Guide to Weaving, Number 3*, Lease Sticks Press, Sausalito CA, 2005
Braiding for fringes: Carey, Jacqui, *The Braider's Bible*, Search Press, Tunbridge Wells, 2007
Procion dyeing: Deighan, Helen, *Dyeing in Plastic Bags*, Crossways Patch, Hindhead, 2007
Indigo: Prideaux, Vivien, *A Handbook of Indigo Dyeing*, Search Press, Tunbridge Wells, 2003

Pattern and symmetry

Ball, Philip, *Shapes*, Oxford University Press, Oxford, 2009
Ball, Philip, *Flow*, Oxford University Press, Oxford, 2009
Ball, Philip, *Branches*, Oxford University Press, Oxford, 2009
du Sautoy, Marcus, *Symmetry*, HarperCollins, New York, 2008
Hanks, David A, *The Decorative Designs of Frank Lloyd Wright*, Dutton, New York, 1979
Hargittai, I and Hargittai, M, *Symmetry*, Shelter, Bolinas CA, 1994
Juniper, Andrew, *Wabi-sabi*, Tuttle, 2003
Stevens, Peter S, *Handbook of Regular Patterns*, MIT Press, Cambridge MA, 1980
Thompson, D'Arcy Wentworth, *On Growth and Form*, Cambridge University Press, Cambridge, 2007
Wade, David, *Symmetry*, Wooden Books, Glastonbury, 2006
Wade, David, *Li*, Wooden Books, Glastonbury, 2007

Colour

Albers, Josef, *Interaction of Color*, Yale University Press, New Haven, (revised) 1975
Chevreul, M E, *The Principles of Harmony and Contrast of Colours*, Schiffer, West Chester PA, (revised) 1987
Menz, Deb, *colorWorks*, Interweave Press, Loveland CO, 2004

Lace

Atkinson, Jane, *Pattern Design for Torchon Lace*, Batsford, London, 1987 (revised 2nd edition on CD-ROM, 2000)
Cook, Bridget M, *Practical Skills in Bobbin Lace*, Batsford, London, 1987
Cook, Bridget M and Stott, Geraldine, *The Book of Bobbin Lace Stitches*, Batsford, 1980
Lohr, Ulrike, *The Beginning of the End*, Frechverlag, Stuttgart, 2000
Nottingham, P, *The Technique of Bobbin Lace*, Batsford, London, 1976
Nottingham, P, *The Technique of Torchon Lace*, Batsford, London, 1979
Novak, Jana, *Borddekoration et al*, Moravia, Harlev, 2000
Robinson, Deborah, *Logarithmic Lace*, The Lace Guild, Stourbridge, 2002
Wade, Elizabeth, Torchon Lacemaking, Crowood Press, Marlborough,1996

Threads

Paternoster, Brenda, *Threads for Lace*, Rochester, (5th edn) 2009
Wolter-Kampmann, Martina, *Faden & Brief*, Dortmund, 1999

Art, artists, Zeitgeist, artefacts

Allthorpe-Guyton, M, Tucker, M and Lampert, C, *Ian McKeever Paintings*, Lund Humphries, Farnham, 2009
De Bono, Edward, *Lateral Thinking*, Penguin, London, 1990
Eames, Elizabeth, *English Medieval Tiles*, British Museum, London, 1985
Edwards, Betty, *Drawing on the Right Side of the Brain*, HarperCollins, London, 1992
Edwards, Betty, *Drawing on the Artist Within*, HarperCollins, London, 1995
Giralt-Miracle, Daniel, *Gaudí: La búsqueda de la forma*, Museu d'Història de la Ciutat, Barcelona, 2002
Gombrich, E, *The Sense of Order*, Phaidon, Oxford, 1979
Hockney, David, *Secret Knowledge*, Thames & Hudson, London, 2006
Holzhey, Magdalena, *Vasarely*, Taschen, Koln, 2005
Krauss, Rosalind, *Grids*, Pace Gallery, New York, 1979
Lewty, Simon, *Writing Silence, The Art of Susan Michie*, Lacerta, 2008
Lippard, Lucy, *Eva Hesse*, Da Capo Press, 1992
MACBA/Hayward Gallery, *Kinetic Art: Force Fields*, MACBA/Hayward Gallery, London, 2000
May, Matthew E, *In Pursuit of Elegance*, Broadway Books
Quinn, Bradley, *Textile Designers at the Cutting Edge*, Laurence King, London, 2009
Roberts, L and Thrift, J, *The Designer and the Grid*, Rotovision, Hove, 2005
Zelevansky, Lynn, *Beyond Geometry*, MIT Press, Cambridge MA, 2004
Zerbst, Rainer, *Antoní Gaudí*, Taschen, Koln, 1991

References

[1] Atkinson, Jane, *Pattern Design for Torchon Lace*, Batsford, 1987 (revised 2nd edition on CD-ROM from www. contemporarylace.com)
[2] Allthorpe-Guyton, M, Tucker M and Lampert, C, *Ian McKeever Paintings*, Lund Humphries, 2009
[3] Krauss, Rosalind, *Grids*, Pace Gallery, 1979
[4] Lippard, Lucy, *Eva Hesse*, Da Capo Press, 1992
[5] Simon Lewty, Writing Silence, *The Art of Susan Michie*, Lacerta, 2008
[6] Gombrich, Ernst, *The Sense of Order*, Phaidon, 1979
[7] Plotadot grids by Deborah Robinson
[8] Robinson, Deborah, *Logarithmic Lace*, The Lace Guild, 2002
[9] du Sautoy, Marcus, *Symmetry*, HarperCollins, 2008
[10] Ball, Philip, *Branches*, Oxford University Press, 2009

Index

First published in Great Britain in 2011
10 9 8 7 6 5 4 3 2 1

ISBN 978-0-9551512-1-7

© Jane Atkinson 2011

The rights of Jane Atkinson to be identified as the author of this work have been asserted by her in accordance with the Copyright, Designs and Patents Act 1988.

Designer: Janet McCallum
Main photography: David Bird
Editor: Katherine James
Production manager: Geoff Barlow
Reproduction by Imagewrite Ltd
Printed and bound in China by WKT

Published by Webfoot Books, 78 Pauntley Road, Christchurch, Dorset BH23 3JW, UK
www.contemporarylace.com
A CIP record is registered and held at the British Library